"Derek and Lindsay Allen have written a creative and important book confronting the reality of cultural Christianity in the South. It is not a harsh or mocking expose from a distance. It is hopeful and written for the people they love and serve. It is their desire to awaken the reality of Christ in the lives of people who are very comfortable in their culture and assume their culture by its very nature is right with God. Derek and Lindsay have a unique perspective as experienced church planters outside of the cultural South. This gives clarity and urgency to their message. With love and humor, this book will challenge your cultural perspective and, by God's grace, help you find the life transforming grace of God in the reality of Jesus without a mullet."

Ed Litton, Pastor, Redemption Church, past SBC President
Kathy Litton, Director of Spouse Development, SEND Network

"Derek and Lindsay have done a masterful job describing many ways we have minimized the effectiveness of living the Christ-Centered life by being so influenced by the secular culture. *Mullet Theology* serves as a convicting resource for all of us. I pray it brings us to the point we beg for forgiveness in our wayward tendencies."

Jim Law, Director of Pastor Relations for North America, NAMB

"For decades cultural Christianity has left a spiritually devastating impact on America, but more so on the Bible Belt of the southeast. Cultural Christianity is a shameful expression of the Christian faith because it is devoid of real repentance. In their book, Mullet Theology, Derek and Lindsay take to task this disingenuous expression of faith with a blend of creative winsomeness and hard-hitting biblical truth. I recommend that you give this book your undivided attention and then pass it on to someone else. And yes, I did have a mullet, but have since regretted the haircut and repented from the hypocrisy of the theology."

Kevin D. Blackwell, PhD, DMin, Assistant to the President for Church Relations Ministry Training Institute, Executive Director Department of Christian Ministry, Samford University

Mullet Theology

How Jesus in the front and party in the back
is killing the soul of the cultural South.

Dr. Derek and Lindsay Allen

Copyright © 2023 by NELLALLEN INC
All rights reserved. This book or any portion thereof may not be reproduced or used in any manner whatsoever without the express written permission of the publisher except for the use of brief quotations in a book review.

Printed in the United States of America
ISBN 979-8-9896458-0-0

NELLALLEN INC
6508 Sugar Creek Drive South
Mobile, AL 36695

www.thec2life.org

Unless otherwise noted, Scripture quotations are from the ESV® Bible (The Holy Bible, English Standard Version®), copyright © 2001 by Crossway, a publishing ministry of Good News Publishers. Used by permission. All rights reserved.

Table of Contents

Introduction: What is Mullet Theology? 1

Chapter One: The Monster Ballad Mullet 5

Chapter Two: The 'Merica Mullet 15

Chapter Three: The Wrastlin' Mullet 23

Chapter Four: The Billy Ray Mullet 33

Chapter Five: The Picture Day Mullet 45

Chapter Six: The Slater Mullet 57

Chapter Seven: The 'Dega Mullet 65

Chapter Eight: The Joe Dirt Mullet 77

Chapter Nine: It's Time for a Haircut 89

Appendix: A Look in the Mirror 101

Introduction: What is Mullet Theology?

"Business in the front, and party in the back." This has been the long-standing mantra of the mullet. This haircut's claim to fame is that you can have it all at the same time. However, one big problem is that life isn't lived as a two-dimensional photograph. In real life, you can't hide the party in the back. Eventually, everyone will know.

Somehow, the mullet continues to survive. It seems like a style that would have died out by now, but it has hung on for decades. Most people think of the mullet as a caricature and a joke. It's the style people boldly wear, then deeply regret.

As people who were born and raised in the monogrammed buckle of the Bible Belt, we (Derek and Lindsay) have observed a deep correlation between this daring hairdo and what is commonly known as cultural Christianity. We've come to call it Mullet Theology. Instead of "business in the front, and party in the back" Mullet Theology is better described as "Jesus in the front, and party in the back." This way of life has just enough "Jesus" to look religious or even Christian to the untrained eye . . . in a photo . . . with the use of optimal lighting. But a closer look reveals the party going on behind those ears. The mullet may be a tragedy of style, but the bigger tragedy is those who are so immersed in cultural Christianity that they have bought into the lie of trying to live in two opposing realities at once. Cultural Christians want the comfort of Jesus *and* the pleasure of living life the way they want. Jesus is just a cute accessory to their lives.

Our hope is that in reading this book, our readers will see that Jesus should *be* everything we want rather than a means to *give us* everything we want. We hope to expose some ugly truths about our own culture while giving real hope to those deceived by its enticing lies.

Overview

Some mullets are more memorable than others. Chances are, you can think of a few famous/infamous mullets. We have chosen a few of our favorites, and we use them as teaching tools to help identify unique characteristics of cultural Christianity. Each chapter is named after a mullet.

>Chapter One: The Monster Ballad Mullet
>Chapter Two: The 'Merica Mullet
>Chapter Three: The Wrastlin' Mullet
>Chapter Four: The Billy Ray Mullet
>Chapter Five: The Picture Day Mullet
>Chapter Six: The Slater Mullet
>Chapter Seven: The 'Dega Mullet
>Chapter Eight: The Joe Dirt Mullet

After we describe each mullet, we get out the trimming tools. What better cutting apparatus than the Sword of the Spirit? It's pretty sharp.

> For the word of God is living and active, sharper than any two-edged sword, piercing to the division of soul and of spirit, of joints and of marrow, and discerning the thoughts and intentions of the heart. **Hebrews 4:12**

Each chapter includes practical tips designed to strengthen your spiritual life and help you live out a more authentic faith. That's our hope and our goal. We want to help you live a more God-honoring, Christ-centered life. The book ends with Chapter Nine: Time for a Haircut. The final chapter is designed to help you take the hard but necessary steps to shape up your theological hairstyle.

Definitions

It might be helpful if we define a few terms before diving in.

Cultural Christianity: a type of pseudo-Christianity based more on the traditions of a culture than the gospel. Cultural Christianity uses biblical language, Christian symbols, and

Christian rituals, but it is severed from the real power of the gospel.

Cultural South: the region of the United States which houses traditional southern culture. The cultural South is located in the geographical south, but not all of the geographical south is part of the cultural South. For instance, Miami, Florida is in the geographical south, but it is not part of the cultural South. There are many ways to distinguish the cultural South from the rest of the United States. Here are a few of our favorites:

- If you can order sweet tea and grits at a restaurant without getting a funny look, you're probably in the cultural South.
- If your grandmother makes better biscuits than Cracker Barrel, she's probably from the cultural South.
- If you think eating healthy means more fried vegetables, you're probably from the cultural South.
- If you watch *Forrest Gump* and don't think it's that strange of a story, you're probably from the cultural South.
- If you're thinking about Jeff Foxworthy right now, you're probably from the cultural South.

Southern Cultural Christianity: the cultural Christianity of the cultural South. It is marked by positive features like conservative politics, conservative morality, strong feelings of patriotism, support for local churches, and support for prayer in public venues. It is also marked by a surface level version of real Christianity. It does not really engage with Scripture, and it does not take discipleship seriously. Its relationship with Jesus is more superficial than serious.

Theological Mullet: any theology or lifestyle that claims some level of allegiance to Jesus while holding onto aspects of an unbiblical lifestyle.

A Warning

Let me warn you. We are pretty honest about cultural Christianity. We love the people and culture of the South. We are both southern born and southern bred. We love the salt of the earth people that call the cultural South home, and we love southern hospitality, southern food, southern traditions, and southern style. We believe the world can learn a lot from the cultural South. But we also believe that every culture has its blind spots. The cultural South is no exception.

Mullet Theology is our attempt to lovingly expose some of the blind spots we see in the culture we call home.

We pray you will be encouraged, challenged, and more like Jesus after reading this book.

Chapter One: The Monster Ballad Mullet

Introduction

"They taught us how to love. They taught us how to live. And now they're back. *Monster Ballads*. Thirty-five hits on two CDs and two cassettes."[1] If you know, you know. If you don't know, then you missed one of the greatest compilation albums in history. *Monster Ballads* was released in 1999 as a two-disc collection of thirty-five power ballads from the late 80s and early 90s. If you're looking for an 80s hair band mullet showcase, look no further than *Monster Ballads*. Bands like Warrant, Whitesnake, Guns and Roses, Cinderella, and Europe had their own style of business in the front and party in the back. They took the mullet to places it had never been before—they permed it and teased it to new heights.

Monster Ballads was filled with entertaining songs from hair bands, but claiming those songs teach us how to love and live is a bit much—or is it? For many people, their philosophy of life and love has been mostly shaped by popular media like power ballads, country classics, R&B, movies, and sitcoms. The result is a Jesus in the front, party in the back view of love, romance, and intimacy.

Behold the bequeathed wisdom of *Monster Ballads*:

---

[1] From the original *Monster Ballads* commercial https://www.youtube.com/watch?v=pNCiXKpO94g.

In "Heaven Isn't Too Far Away", Warrant teaches that Heaven can be accessed when a man is his girlfriend's hero and when she is his biggest fan.[2] "When I See You Smile" by Bad English exclaims the power of one look, one touch, and one smile from a lover. According to the song, it's all you'll ever need, and nothing else in the world can come close to that kind of power.[3] In "This Could be the Night", Loverboy assures us that one night of lovemaking could be the night to end all nights.[4] REO Speedwagon teaches that some feelings are so strong they cannot be resisted. We must give up and give in to our feelings. That's the message of "Can't Fight This Feeling."[5] In "Take Me Home Tonight," Eddie Money describes sexual arousal as a clear sign that the woman causing the arousal is "the answer."[6]

Did you notice the incongruence between *Monster Ballads*' view of love and romance and Scripture's view of love and romance? It should be obvious, but if your view of love and romance has been shaped by the Monster Ballad Mullet, it might be hard to see the difference. The reality is that Christians in the cultural South often align themselves more with popular media's thoughts on love and romance than scriptural principles.

Mullet Description

The Monster Ballad Mullet embodies American music and media's ideas about love, romance, and relationships. This mullet elevates romantic feelings and sexual chemistry above commitment and biblical, sacrificial love. The Monster Ballad Mullet puts Jesus in the front by talking about love and marriage, which are biblical concepts, but keeps the party in the back by bankrupting the biblical concepts and redefining them to be synonymous with the ideas of the culture.

Peruse American media. What message does it communicate about love and romance? Love is a feeling, even more, it is a rush of emotions. It's exciting and electrifying. There's no feeling like it, and once true love is found, it must be pursued at all costs. Boundaries

---

[2] Warrant, "Heaven Isn't Too Far Away," Disc 1, Track 1, *Monster Ballads*, Razor and Tie, 1999, CD.
[3] Bad English, "When I See You Smile," Disc 1, Track 3, *Monster Ballads*, Razor and Tie, 1999, CD.
[4] Loverboy, "This Could Be the Night," Disc 1, Track 14, *Monster Ballads*, Razor and Tie, 1999, CD.
[5] REO Speedwagon, "Can't Fight This Feeling," Disc 1, Track 13, *Monster Ballads*, Razor and Tie, 1999, CD.
[6] Eddie Money, "Take Me Home Tonight/Be My Baby," Disc 2, Track 17, *Monster Ballads*, Razor and Tie, 1999, CD.

must not stop true love. Tradition must not stop true love. Morality must not stop true love. In fact, denying true love is immoral above all else.

What does the Monster Ballad Mullet teach us about sex? Sex is the ultimate expression of true love, and it is the ultimate human experience. That is, of course, if you are having sex with the right person. And how can you know if you're having sex with the right person? Just ask, "Is sex the ultimate experience for me?" If not, then you're not having sex with the right person! If the spark is gone, it's time to move on.

Roxette didn't make the *Monster Ballads* album, but the 1980s rock duo captures the spirit of the Monster Ballad Mullet in two songs. First, "It Must Have Been Love" teaches that love comes and goes. It's like the flowing water or the blowing wind. Passionate feelings must mean love, and when those passionate feelings are gone, so is love.[9] Second, "Listen to Your Heart" promotes the heart as the ultimate guide. Listening to your heart, according to Roxette, is all you can do in difficult relationship situations.[10]

Of course, this is SO FAR from the biblical prescription for love and sex. But be honest, which philosophy—Roxette or Jesus—has a stronger hold on culture? Which philosophy permeates the hearts and minds of many who attend church in the cultural South on a regular basis?

Mullet Sightings

Take a look around—this mullet is everywhere in the cultural South! So many people who claim to be Christ followers **give advice about love, romance, and marriage that is more aligned with the culture than with Christ.** So the presentation is Jesus in the front, but when the rubber meets the road, it's party in the back.

Church goers and cultural Christians in the southern United States have completely bought the lie that love is an intense emotion. Teenagers and young adults in the cultural South are encouraged to search for intense emotional feelings of connection. And they let those feelings fuel critical life decisions, like who to have sex with, who to marry, and whether to stay married or get divorced.

---

[9] Roxette, "It Must Have Been Love," Track 1, *It Must Have Been Love*, EMI Group Limited, 1987, Cassette.
[10] Roxette, "Listen to Your Heart," Track 12, *Look Sharp!*, EMI Group Limited, 1988, Cassette.

Of course, these same messages are heard outside the cultural South, but what makes us different is our Mullet Theology. We put the Jesus up front to hide the party in the back. In the cultural South, these unbiblical ideas about love and romance might come straight from a committed church member, deacon, small group leader, or even a pastor at a church which prides itself on being "conservative" and committed to the Bible.

Teenagers are encouraged to "date" and establish long-term relationships in search of true love. Those in their early twenties are conditioned to look for Mr. or Mrs. Right. And how will they know? They'll just know. Or, as Roxette might say, "Listen to your heart." **Love will guide the way through emotional connection and physical chemistry.** Of course, physical chemistry will lead to physical intimacy like sensual touching, heavy kissing, and even touching in sexual areas. Actual intercourse, according to the Monster Ballad Mullet, should be saved for marriage, or at least someone you know for sure you really love. After all, Jesus must be in the front. Those are the messages the cultural Christian South sells its teenagers and young adults.

It should not be a surprise that after marriage the Monster Ballad Mullet messaging continues. Sexual attraction often decreases after marriage, which is a direct result of buying the cultural messaging about love, romance, and sex. When sexual desire and fulfillment decrease, the pressure is on for one or both spouses to do something to increase sexual desire. Perhaps the husband should be more romantic, or maybe the wife needs to update her personal appearance. That will fix the relationship because, after all, this mullet teaches that love and sex are all about connection and attraction.

Many marriages just can't get the spark back, and that's when the Monster Ballad Mullet strikes again, "I just don't have feelings for him/her anymore." This feelings-first philosophy is rampant throughout western civilization, but what makes it unique in the cultural South is that it is found among those who claim to be sold-out Christ followers. In fact, in the cultural South, it's highly likely that a professing Christian will give the Monster Ballad Mullet advice, **"You need to do what makes you happy. If you're not happy, he/she is not right for you. If you're not happy, why would you stay in a loveless marriage?"** Because it's the scriptural, gospel-centered, Christ-honoring thing to do! But more on that in a moment.

Mullet Dangers

Some of the dangers of the Monster Ballad Mullet should be obvious, but then again, it's possible that the cultural South has hidden the party in the back with the Jesus in the front for so long that many are blind to the danger. The Monster Ballad Mullet leads to broken marriages, broken homes, and empty, unfulfilled lives.

Before marriage, young adults, teenagers, and even children buy into the lie that they should be in search of "true love." They believe it alone will bring them the deepest satisfaction possible. Ironically, they are urged and cheered on in their task by adults who, in many cases, haven't felt a spark of emotional or romantic connection in a long time. It seems the only hope some adults have of feeling the thrill of "love" is to live vicariously through the romantic pursuits of the younger generation.

The Monster Ballad Mullet also hijacks your God-given purpose. Let's do a little experiment. Do you know any of the words to these popular love songs?

"Can't Help Falling in Love" by Elvis Presley

"Take My Breath Away" by Berlin

"My Heart Will Go On" by Celine Dion

"Crazy In Love" by Beyonce

How did you do? Chances are you can sing lines from most of these love songs.

Now for the second part of the experiment. Do you know the answer to this question: What is the chief end of man? Have you ever heard that question? It's the first question in both the Larger and Shorter Westminster Catechisms.[12] The answer is "The chief end of man is to glorify God and enjoy Him forever." Most Christians in the cultural South have lines from the top twenty loves songs of all time embedded in their memory, but solid theology[13] is foreign to them.

---

[12] The Larger Westminster Catechism can be found at http://www.freepresbyterian.org/uploads/Larger_Catechism.pdf.
[13] We do not agree with everything in the Westminster Catechisms, which is why we are not Presbyterian. The point is, however, that Christians in the cultural South are more aware of the culture's views on almost every subject than they are of biblical and theological principles regarding those same subjects.

Christian marriage, and the process leading to it, should look very different from the rest of the world. When we take the same approach as the majority of those around us, we cannot be shocked when we get the same results, or even worse.

You've probably heard the divorce rate among Christians is the same as that of non-Christians. A closer look at the data reveals that is not exactly true. Professor Bradley Wright, a sociologist at the University of Connecticut, analyzed Christian marriages and found that sixty percent of those who identify as Christians but rarely attend church have been divorced. Of those who attend church regularly, only thirty-eight percent have been divorced.[14]

Another sociologist, W. Bradford Wilcox, found that culturally conservative Protestant Christians are twenty percent *more* likely to divorce, compared to secular Americans.[15] However, he found that "active conservative Protestants" who regularly attend church are thirty-five percent *less likely to divorce* compared to those who have no religious affiliation. In other words, those who are only cultural Christians actually divorce at higher rates than non-Christians. But Christians who are active in their faith experience divorce less often. Other studies have confirmed the divorce rates of committed Christian believers are not identical to the general population—not even close. Being a committed, faithful believer makes a measurable difference in marriage.[16]

Mullet Makeover: Christ-Centered Principles to Reshape Your Theology

Have you ever seen a picture of a band that was popular in your teenage years and wondered, "What happened to them?!" Just as the years reveal the imperfections and fragility of rock stars, so too the Monster Ballad Mullet looks a little wrinkled and saggy after time takes its toll. Here are some Christ-centered principles that will never succumb to the negative effects of aging. In fact, they get better with time.

---

[14] Bradley R. E. Wright, *Christians Are Hate-Filled Hypocrites . . . and Other Lies You've Been Told* (Minneapolis, MN: Bethany House, 2010), 133.
[15] W. Bradford Wilcox and Elizabeth Williamson, "The Cultural Contradictions of Mainline Family Ideology and Practice," *American Religions and the Family*, ed. Don S. Browning and David A. Clairmont (New York: Columbia University Press, 2007), 50.
[16] https://www.focusonthefamily.com/marriage/divorce-rate-in-the-church-as-high-as-the-world/.

Submit to Christ, Not Your feelings

Feelings change. That's what they do. Within just an hour's time we could feel hot then cold, hungry then full, peaceful then annoyed, comfortable then that weird tingly feeling you get when your leg is going to sleep, and the list goes on and on. But Jesus . . . Scripture tells us that "Jesus Christ is the same yesterday and today and forever" (Hebrews 13:8). Because of this beautiful truth, we can trust Him. He is the Way, the Truth, and the Life. If He was ever the Way, He is always the Way. When we need a Way to follow because we feel lost, it's Him. If He was ever the Truth, He is always the Truth. When we are looking for Truth because we feel confused, it's Him. If He was ever the Life, He is always the Life. When we need life because we feel dead, it's Him. If He was ever trustworthy, He is always trustworthy. When we don't know what to believe, we can trust what He says is best, really is best.

Learn Life-Giving Truths by Repeating Them Over, and Over, and Over, and . . .

Decrease your intake of flesh-feeding ideas and increase the intake of soul-feeding truth. Hillary Ferrer, author of *Mama Bear Apologetics: Guide to Sexuality* points out that "our brains have a hard time distinguishing between that which is familiar and that which is true."[17] In other words, if you hear something over and over and over again, you start to just accept it as truth. What are we repeating in our minds through what we take in time after time after time? Take some steps to fill your ears, mind, heart, and soul with truth from God's Word so you can better recognize the lies that try to creep in.

Some practical ways to do this are:

Regularly attend worship and small group, and serve at your local church.

Change your playlist to songs that have rich theology.

Fill your home with meaningful Scripture passages through artwork, chalkboards, or sticky notes.

Use filtering services like Vidangel or Clearplay when watching shows or movies at home.

Use filters on your devices like Covenant Eyes, Netsanity, or Accountable2You to increase accountability across all devices.

---

[17] https://www.radicalradiance.live/podcast-episodes/hillarymorganferrer.

Use pluggedin.com to help determine if a movie or show is appropriate to view.

Frequent sites like desiringgod.org or thegospelcoalition.org to access articles, sermons, and podcasts that can help deepen your understanding of Scripture and application thereof.

Speaking of podcasts, may we suggest our own, *The Christ Centered Life* podcast? We cover many topics and work to help listeners form a Christ-centered worldview.

Throw away the smutty romance novels and read books that will inspire authentic Christ-like love.

Use tools like the Fighter Verses app, a journal, or notecards to help you memorize Scripture. After all, God says memorizing Scripture helps us avoid sinning against Him![18]

Love with Your Actions, Not Just Your Heart

What does God have to say about love, romance, and marriage His way? He has so much to say! In fact, it would take volumes of books to address, but a good start would be the entire fifth chapter of the book of Ephesians. A few principles found in this chapter are: be imitators of God (v. 1), walk in sacrificial love (v. 2), don't even entertain discussions about sexual immorality (v. 3), avoid crude jokes and foolish talk (v. 4), try to discern what is pleasing to God (v. 10), expose works of darkness rather than taking part in them (v. 11), make the best use of your time (v. 16), do not be drunk but be filled with the Spirit (v. 18), encourage each other with spiritual songs (v. 19), make melody to the Lord with your heart (v. 19), and be thankful to Him for everything (v. 20). Many of these truths help build a healthy foundation for the individual believer so they are ready to be a life-giving partner to their spouse in marriage.

The remainder of the chapter gives very specific instructions to husbands and wives. It boils down to this: wives, submit to your own husbands, as to the Lord (v. 22), and respect your husband (v. 33). Husbands, love your wives, as Christ loved the church and gave Himself up for her (v. 25) and love your wife as you do yourself (v. 33). It is a time-tested formula, and it works. When a husband loves his wife sacrificially as Christ loved the church, he daily gives himself up for her, and he cares for her as much as he does his own self. It is very easy to submit to that kind of man. When a wife submits to and respects her

---

[18] Psalm 119:11

husband, as to the Lord, it is very easy to love that kind of woman sacrificially.

We like to say it this way when giving advice to young couples entering marriage: spend your marriage working to out-serve the other person. Aren't you grateful that Jesus's love for humanity wasn't the twenty-first century version of feelings-based love? If Jesus had waited to show His greatest love for us when we made Him feel all the feels inside, it never would have happened. No, the Bible tells us that

> God shows His love for us in that while we were still sinners, Christ died for us. **Romans 5:8**

That is action-based love. He made the choice to do it based on God's purposes and plan, not feelings. We can do the same through the power the Holy Spirit gives to us. Jesus said it this way:

> Greater love has no one than this, that someone lay down his life for his friends. You are my friends if you do what I command you. **John 15:13–14**

You've probably heard the first part of that passage, but the second is less popular. We like to think about the great love of Jesus when He laid down His life for us. And yes, that is an amazing truth. The primary context, however, is that Jesus is calling us to show Him love by laying down our life for Him. How? Obey Him. We show Him, and others, love by actions of obedience to Him. When your husband is not acting respectable, you can still respect him because Jesus earned that respect on his behalf. Do it for Jesus if for no other reason. When your wife is not acting very loveable, you can still love her and give yourself up for her because Jesus earned that love on her behalf. Christian love is not a matter of paying it back. It's a matter of paying it forward.

Chapter Two: The 'Merica Mullet

Introduction

      According to dictionary.com's slang dictionary, 'Merica (also spelled Murica) came to cultural prominence in the early 2000s as a derogatory term to mock patriotism, Second Amendment supporters, and Republican political policies. Like many such terms, those it was first used to insult embraced the term. Now 'Merica is used by God-and-country-loving people across the United States to express patriotism and national pride.[19]

      And nothing goes with patriotism, Second Amendment rights, and national pride like—you guessed it—mullets! Just search the internet for "'Merica Mullet," and you'll find:

      An eagle sporting an American flag bandana and a mullet

      A hat with 'Merica in red, white, and blue across the front and a built in mullet wig

      Multiple mullet-brandishing patriots with American flags shaved into the "business" section of the mullet

      Now, let me be clear—we love America! The United States has done more to increase liberty, prosperity, and quality of life for people of all types and from all spheres of the planet than any other nation in

---

[19] https://www.dictionary.com/e/slang/murica/.

history. The USA is not perfect, but neither is Chile, China, or the Czech Republic. America's past is checkered with injustices, but so is that of Iceland, India, Indonesia, and Ireland. American actions have caused environmental damage, but so have those of Mexico, Moldova, and Monaco. Native Americans were displaced by settlers, but the same thing occurred many times throughout history in Nepal, Nicaragua, New Zealand, and the Netherlands. US military campaigns have sometimes harmed innocent people, but so have those of the UK, Ukraine, Uganda, and Uruguay. Businessmen from America propagated and profited from the slave trade, but so did businessmen from Zimbabwe and Zambia.

We love America, and to be honest, there's a part of us that swells up with pride when we think about 'Merica. But as followers of Christ, our primary citizenship is not in the United States of America. Our greatest allegiance and primary citizenship belongs to the Kingdom of the Lord Jesus Christ. Sometimes, that concept can get lost in the Christian cultural South.

Mullet Description

The 'Merica Mullet equates being American with being Christian. It gives primary allegiance to secondary citizenship. The 'Merica Mullet keeps Jesus in the front by attending church, supporting conservative morality, and preserving traditional religious expressions in the culture, such as prayer in the public sphere. The party in the back reveals that Jesus and His Kingdom priorities and principles actually take second place to preserving and prospering the good ol' US of A. It stands with the red, white, and blue even when it has abandoned the God of the Bible and His teachings. It chokes up at the thought of all the soldiers who died for our country's freedoms, but is apathetic and bored with worshiping the Savior who died for the ultimate freedom for all mankind.

Mullet Sightings

This mullet can be tricky to detect at times because at first glance it just looks like simple patriotism. After all, The United States of America was founded on so many biblical principles and ideals. It was started and led by mostly Christian men and women seeking the opportunity to live in a land that would allow them to worship freely. These factors can make it seem only right to elevate our nation above all others. However, we have seen evidence from the beginning that this nation, as great as it has been, is not Heaven. It is not the eternal sinless dwelling place of God and His saints. Americans are not God's chosen people.

Idols are good things that make lousy gods. That's what happens with the 'Merica Mullet. As Christians, we should be thankful for the ways in which America is good, and even the ways in which America is great—exceptional, unmatched. It is a good thing to be proud of those who have demonstrated Christ-likeness by sacrificing for the good of others. Healthy national pride turns into a 'Merica Mullet when someone can **passionately sing "God Bless the USA" complete with tears, yet remain lifeless and unemotional when singing about Jesus.**

Another mark of the 'Merica Mullet is when someone **acts as if America is our promised land, and a politician is our savior.** This happens on both sides of the aisle. In recent presidential election cycles we've witnessed those on the left attach messianic level expectations to figures like Barak Obama and those on the right do so with Donald Trump.

It's time to have an honest discussion. We doubt that anyone reading this book got caught up in the "Obama is our savior" hype. That's not as big of a temptation for our tribe. Many within conservative evangelical circles, however, jumped in with both feet for Trump. To lay all of our cards on the table, both of us (Derek and Lindsay) voted for Donald Trump in 2016 and 2020. If we are faced with a decision between Joe Biden and Donald Trump in 2024, we will vote for Trump again. BUT, Donald Trump is not our savior. And he's not the savior of our nation.

Unfortunately, many of the 'Merica Mullet wearers not only look past the countless sinful words and actions of Donald Trump, they also run to the microphone to defend them. We appreciate many of the changes Trump made during his presidency, including appointing pro-life Supreme Court justices Gorsuch, Kavanaugh, and Barrett. We are grateful for his policies on border control and his desire to surround himself with people who would pray for him. On the other hand, we are not going to pretend that he is in any way a person showing fruit bearing with repentance. When a person says they have never asked for forgiveness because they "don't want to bring God into the picture,"[20] they clearly have not understood the story Romans 3:23 tells. We are talking about a man who said, "I like to be good. I don't

---

[20] https://www.cnn.com/2015/07/18/politics/trump-has-never-sought-forgiveness/index.html.

like to have to ask for forgiveness. And I am good. I don't do a lot of things that are bad. I try to do nothing that is bad."

Trump looked back on his life and described it this way, "My life was so great in so many ways. The business was so great . . . a beautiful girlfriend, a beautiful wife, a beautiful everything. Life was just a bowl of cherries."[21] We do understand that many of these interviews and articles were used by Donald Trump's opposition to try to deter him from being elected, but they didn't force him to say these things. It was his actual words in context, not coerced.

This is only the beginning of Trump's words and actions that do not in any way reflect Christ-like character. The purpose of this chapter, however, is not to attack Trump. Remember, we voted for him and will do so again if he is the Republican nominee. The issue with the 'Merica Mullet is not that a politician has sin in his past or even present. The issue is that the 'Merica Mullet ignores, or in some cases, justifies sin, not calling it out for what it is. Why? The agenda is too important, and in their judgment, the end justifies the means. That's just not biblical ethics.

For some Christians, Trump has an almost siren song effect that puts people in a kind of weird trance. They've bought into the Trump branding and messaging with little or no discernment. In the worst cases, they've attached prophetic importance to Trump's presidency. Because they are so committed to Trump, they are quick to defend his actions even when they are clearly sinful and inexcusable. The phenomenon prevents them from being able to objectively evaluate and separate the good from the bad. The 'Merica Mullet seems incapable of celebrating Trump's positive actions while at the same time holding him accountable for negative and sinful behavior.

The 'Merica Mullet didn't begin with Trump's campaign for the 2016 Republican presidential nomination. The 'Merica Mullet has been around for decades. It lives for the "good ol' days" rather than Thy Kingdom come Thy will be done. The 'Merica Mullet sees America as the new Israel and refuses to believe any nation could be used by God in an equal or greater way. It cannot imagine that America does not play a key role in the future unfolding of God's Kingdom. The 'Merica Mullet sees the good God has used America to accomplish in the world and supposes we have set the gold standard for God-honoring nations.

---

[21] https://www.nydailynews.com/news/politics/trump-cheating-ivana-marla-beautiful-1994-article-1.2822695.

What if the return of Jesus is delayed for another 1,000 years and America becomes nothing more than a chapter in the history books? If that seems unimaginable to you, it might evidence of the 'Merica Mullet. Can God use us to accomplish His purposes? Of course. In fact, He will use us to accomplish His purposes just as He has used the nations of Europe, the Roman Empire, the Greek Empire, the Persian Empire, the Babylonian Empire, the Assyrian Empire, the Egyptian Empire, and every person, city, nation, and region throughout all of human history. History is His story. There are only two special groups about which God has made specific promises—the nation of Israel and the church. That's it. America did not make the list.

Does that mean we can't be used by God in a special way? Of course not. As we follow Jesus and submit to His rule, God will bless and use us. The hope for the world, however, is not America and American ideals. The hope for America is Jesus and His Kingdom. The 'Merica Mullet confuses those.

Mullet Dangers

So what's the big deal? The big deal is all the passion, emotion, gratitude, and trust being placed in all the wrong places. Simply put, the 'Merica Mullet gives worship-level praise to people and places not worthy of worship. God alone is worthy of our worship, and anytime we give it to something or someone else, we are robbing God of His glory. The 'Merica Mullet hyper focuses on political parties, overemphasizes patriotism in worship service settings that should be reserved for the glory of God alone, and puts its hope in politicians and policies rather than in Christ and His plan. The danger is idolatry, which breaks the first two of the Ten Commandments.

Mullet Makeover: Christ-Centered Principles to Reshape Your Theology

Maybe God has used this chapter to show you that the 'Merica Mullet is a real thing for you. Maybe He has broken your heart and helped you see the idolatry that was hidden in it. If so, our hope is that you repent, take America and its leaders (past, present, and future) off of the throne of your heart and return Christ to His rightful place. Here are some Christ-centered principles that can decorate the walls of your heart much better than red, white, and blue ever could.

Any Good We See in America is a Gift of God's Grace, and He is Not Obligated to Maintain That Grace for Any Amount of Time

It is not sinful to recognize the good things in our lives like freedom, prosperity, and justice. What is sinful is when we attribute those gifts to men and women as the provider rather than the Creator God.

> Every good gift and every perfect gift is from above, coming down from the Father of lights, with whom there is no variation or shadow due to change. **James 1:17**

If we have freedom, it is only because the God who frees has granted it to us. If we have prosperity, it is only because God the Provider has given it to us. If we have justice, it is only because God the Just has bestowed it upon us. There is assuredly a time and place for showing gratitude for those who were a part of that process. Scripture speaks about honoring the honorable, so we are in no way saying it is sinful to appreciate and celebrate the honorable men and women from present time all the way back to the Magna Carta and beyond who have played a part in shaping this nation. The shift has to be in recognizing the Source of it all, and He must be the ultimate recipient of our thanks and worship.

The other side of this coin is the reality that God may choose, for purposes known only to Him, to withdraw from America the blessings He has given us in the past. We may experience, as we already have in some ways, losses in freedom, prosperity, and justice. The 'Merica Mullet lies about this. It says God would never do that, but He has not promised us external peace and prosperity this side of Heaven. We have to be so careful not to put promises in God's mouth. Doing so makes Him appear to be a liar when those promises are not fulfilled. We must be resolved to follow the Lord in obedience and faithfulness whether our government does or not. We must petition God on our nation's behalf with the motive of seeing souls come to Christ and not merely for the amplification of the Stars and Stripes. What if our nation collapsed or was conquered, but in the process a great revival reached millions of souls? The 'Merica Mullet can't entertain that kind of thought because it subjects the Creator God of the universe to a lesser status subservient to its false god.

Our Allegiance is to Jesus, and Our Worship Service is for His Glory

There is only one Hero in God's story of humanity. There is only One man who lived a perfect life and made a perfect sacrifice. There is only One who offers forgiveness of sin and eternal life for any who will claim it. His name is Jesus. We owe Him everything. He deserves our full affections, attention, obedience, service, allegiance, worship, and praise. When we gather as His people each week, that time should be one hundred percent focused on worshiping God the Father, Jesus Christ the Son, and the Holy Spirit. There are many ways the 'Merica Mullet tries to pull our focus away from Jesus. As much as possible, the focus of our worship services must match the three Sunday school answers we often talk about: God, Jesus, and the Bible.

Churches, let us use the precious time we have set aside for weekly worship be about Jesus, not a nation, not politicians, not even founding documents or sacrificial soldiers. These are things we thank God for, but none of them deserve the glory due to Him. Let us use the breath He gave us to worship Him. Let us pray on behalf of our nation. Such prayers should be prayers of thanksgiving and petitions for blessings. They should also include prayers of repentance for national sins and prayers of humble dependance on God. Mostly, let us pray for the salvation of the American people and the election of righteous men and women to positions of influence and leadership. And let our prayers for our nation be coupled with prayers for the nations—prayers for provision, for justice, for blessings, and mostly for salvation. Let our hearts ache most, not for the return of days gone by in our secondary kingdom, but for the advancement of that nation to which we primarily belong—the Kingdom of our Lord and His Christ.

Only Heaven is Our Promised Land, and Only Jesus is Our Savior

The American Dream, in many ways, is our futile attempt to create Heaven on Earth. The problem is, of course, sin. Heaven is the sinless dwelling place of God. Earth is the sin-broken dwelling place of man. One day, God will change that narrative, but until then, we must set our hearts on our real home. As C. S. Lewis reminds us:

> A continual looking forward to the eternal world is not (as some modern people think) a form of escapism or wishful thinking, but one of the things a Christian is meant to do. It does not mean that we are to leave the present world as it is. If you read history you will find that the Christians who did most for the present world were just those who thought most of the next. The Apostles themselves, who set on foot the conversion of the Roman Empire, the great men who built up the Middle Ages, the English Evangelicals who abolished the Slave Trade, all left their mark on Earth, precisely because their minds were occupied with Heaven. It is since Christians have largely ceased to think of the other world that they have become so

ineffective in this one. Aim at Heaven and you will get earth 'thrown in': aim at earth and you will get neither.[22]

Some have said Christians can be so heavenly minded that they are of no earthly good, but I think John Piper has it right.

> Yes, I know. It is possible to be so heavenly minded that we are of no earthly use. My problem is: I've never met one of those people. And I suspect, if I met one, the problem would not be that his mind is full of the glories of heaven, but that his mind is empty and his mouth is full of platitudes. I suspect that for every professing believer who is useless in this world because of other-worldliness, there are a hundred who are useless because of this-worldliness.[23]

With our sights on Heaven, we will not tempted to settle for the cheap shadow below. Long for Heaven because God is there and sin is not.

---

[22] C. S. Lewis, *Mere Christianity*, Harper Edition (San Francisco: HarperSanFrancisco, 2001), 134-135.

[23] https://www.thegospelcoalition.org/blogs/justin-taylor/so-heavenly-minded-youre-no-earthly-good/.

Chapter Three: The Wrastlin' Mullet

Introduction

As a father, part of my (Derek's) job is to pass wisdom along to the next generation. On more than one occasion, I've explained to my children the difference between wrastlin' and wrestling. "Wrastlin' is a sport where contestants use a combination of punching, kicking, throwing, choking, and aerial acrobatics to subdue their opponents and hold them down for a three count. Wrestling is that fake stuff they do at the Olympics."

It's a joke! I know pro wrestling is fake, but boy, can it be entertaining. I'm not talking about the last twenty years or so in which pro wrestling has become so vulgar and sexualized that no serious follower of Christ has any business watching it. I'm talking about the good ol' days of Andre the Giant, Hulk Hogan (the 80s and 90s version), the Ultimate Warrior, Rowdy Rody Piper, and of course Macho Man Randy Savage.

The 1980s were the zenith of mullets in pro wrestling. If you didn't have a mullet in the 80s, it was probably best that you just stay out of the ring. Those of you who were fans of pro wrestling in those days will remember Jake the Snake Roberts. He was known for two things—bringing a python into the ring, and rocking a world class mullet! Jake the Snake was the standard bearer for pro wrestling mullets.

The Wrastlin' Mullet doesn't have anything to do with whether or not you're a fan of pro wrestling. It's about the character traits promoted and portrayed by wrestlers, and those traits extend well beyond the ring. Pro wrestlers make their living on big personalities and even bigger egos. There is no room for love, joy, peace, patience, kindness, goodness, faithfulness, gentleness, and self-control in the ring. In victory, wrestlers run to the microphone to flaunt their greatness. In defeat, they run to the same microphone to talk about revenge. If you don't believe me, just search for Mean Gene Okerlund interviews.

And then there are the villains. Wrestling fans love to hate the villains, and the villains love to be hated. To stay in the spotlight of the storyline the villains of wrestling lie, cheat, run from a fair fight, and they make deals and back out on them. They play by the rules when the referees are looking, but as soon as the referee is distracted, they cheat to win.

I'll never forget piling into our family living room with all of my friends to watch WCW Superbrawl. While all of this was great entertainment for me and my friends, the "wrastlers" certainly did not reflect Christlikeness. If we aren't careful, however, we can be shaped more into the image of Macho Man Randy Savage than the image of Christ.

Mullet Description

Loud, proud, and unwilling to change, this mullet takes the "I am who I am, now deal with it" approach to life. The Wrastlin' Mullet keeps Jesus in the front by going to church, listening to sermons, and agreeing with sermons on humility, gentleness, and self-control. The party in the back, however, refuses to actually change to be more Christlike. Like a wrestler who follows the rules when the ref is looking but brings in a chair as soon as he turns his back, this mullet puts on a show pretending to be on the straight and narrow in front of the pastor or church leaders, but as soon as the church folks aren't looking, the ugly truth comes out.

Mullet Sightings

How can you recognize this mullet? There are a few catchphrases that give it away in less than three taps. The first few have to do with how the person speaks or behaves. They justify their obnoxious behavior with statements like, **"I just tell it like it is," "That's just who I am, and you'll have to deal with it,"** or **"I ain't**

gonna change for nobody." These attitudes are all completely opposite of the picture Scripture paints for followers of Jesus. Consider just a few examples:

> And if anyone would sue you and take your tunic, let him have your cloak as well. And if anyone forces you to go one mile, go with him two miles. Give to the one who begs from you, and do not refuse the one who would borrow from you. You have heard that it is said, 'You shall love your neighbor and hate your enemy.' But I say to you, love your enemies and pray for those who persecute you. **Matthew 5:40–44**

> So whatever you wish that others would do to you, do also to them. **Matthew 7:12**

> Love is patient and kind; love does not envy or boast; it is not arrogant or rude. It does not insist on its own way; it is not irritable or resentful; it does not rejoice at wrongdoing, but rejoices with the truth. Love bears all things, believes all things, hopes all things, endures all things. **1 Corinthians 13:4–7**

> For you were called to freedom, brothers. Only do not use your freedom as an opportunity for the flesh, but through love serve one another. **Galatians 5:13**

> Be kind to one another, tenderhearted, forgiving one another, as God in Christ forgave you. **Ephesians 4:32**

> Put on then, as God's chosen ones, holy and beloved, compassionate hearts, kindness, humility, meekness, and patience, bearing with one another and, if one has a complaint against another, forgiving each other; as the Lord has forgiven you, so you also must forgive. **Colossians 3:12–13**

> She opens her mouth with wisdom, and the teaching of kindness is on her tongue. **Proverbs 31:26**

Another set of phrases that identify the Wrastlin' Mullet sounds something like this: **"I'll send my money across the world so people can hear about Jesus, but I won't move my rear end three feet down the pew for the same reason."** This is the attitude of many who fill the pews of our churches. They write a check to do their part, but they fail to see the opportunities given to them every week to live missionally.

The Wrastlin' Mullet is not a big fan of growth. Why? It requires change. Growth requires change, and change always leads to conflict. Now that's what the Wrastlin' Mullet was born for—conflict. Just as the Wrastlin' Mullet resists individual change, it resists changes in the church. It could be called the "We've never done it that way, the old carpet is just fine, what's wrong with the 1957 hymnal" Mullet, but that title was a little too long. When the church is growing or trying to grow, and that growth requires church members to make sacrifices like giving up their seat in worship, singing a song that might not be their favorite, or parking a little further from the door, the Wrastlin' Mullet is ready to rumble. Instead of "I'm coming for you this Monday, brother!", the Wrastlin' Mullet often works behind the scenes to undermine pastors and other leaders. Ask any pastor who has been in ministry for more than six months, and chances are, they've encountered some form of the Wrastlin' Mullet.

Mullet Dangers

Instead of producing the fruit of the Spirit, the Wrastlin' Mullet yields a product that looks more like dried spiritual fruit, or even worse, plastic spiritual fruit. From a distance, it might seem real, but the longer you look and the closer you get, the more it becomes apparent that the fruit is fake. Scripture describes the fruit of the Spirit.

> The fruit of the Spirit is love, joy, peace, patience, kindness, goodness, faithfulness, gentleness, self-control; against such things there is no law. And those who belong to Christ Jesus have crucified the flesh with its passions and desires.
> **Galatians 5:22–24**

If the fruit of the Spirit is not coming out, the Holy Spirit is not in control of that person's life. This is dangerous because the fruit we produce as believers is one of the best ways to assess the health of our relationship with the Lord. When our fruit looks more like raisins, it reveals a deeper problem . . . a serious problem. It is a sad thing to see a person who is withering spiritually with no desire to be renewed. It's like watching someone with an eating disorder continue in their sickness, refusing help and wasting away to bones.

The Wrastlin' Mullet is also a breeding ground for missional apathy. It's not really interested in serving and reaching those who don't know Jesus. It cares more about comfort, preferences, or attention getting than the Kingdom. The church needs each believer to be a healthy functioning part of the body so the entire body works well.

For as in one body we have many members, and the members do not all have the same function, so we, though many, are one body in Christ, and individually members one of another. Having gifts that differ according to the grace given to us, let us use them. **Romans 12:4–6**

Speaking the truth in love, we are to grow up in every way into him who is the head, into Christ, from whom the whole body, joined and held together by every joint with which it is equipped, when each part is working properly, makes the body grow so that it builds itself up in love. **Ephesians 4:15–16**

Self-centeredness has no place in the Kingdom of God. We have been designed to work together like individual parts of a single body. That leads to the growth of the whole body, making each individual part healthier and more effective than it would be alone. The God of the universe has predestined His people to be conformed into the image of Jesus, and He won't accept the shallow excuse of "that's just how I am. Deal with it."

Mullet Makeover: Christ-Centered Principles to Reshape Your Theology

Maybe you've found yourself in the middle of a ring with a Wrastlin' Mullet on your head. Here are some ways to tap out and pursue a better path. Consider these tips a way to tap out and let the God of the universe finish the fight (see what we did there?).

Tame Your Tongue

Let me be clear, we are not saying, "Just use nicer words." Nice words are great, but our words come from our hearts, and reveal something much deeper. So just trying to bite your tongue and replace a few words without actually changing what is inside of your heart will only leave you frustrated and exhausted.

"Either make the tree good and its fruit good, or make the tree bad and its fruit bad, for the tree is known by its fruit. You brood of vipers! How can you speak good, when you are evil? For out of the abundance of the heart the mouth speaks. The good person out of his good treasure brings forth good, and the evil person out of his evil treasure brings forth evil. I tell you, on the day of judgment people will give account for every careless word they speak, for by your words you will be

justified, and by your words you will be condemned.".
Matthew 12:33–37

How can we make our hearts good so that our words will be good? Charlie White, who blogs at Mississippimom.com says it this way, "What you soak up, eventually shows up."[24] The fruit from our lips is directly connected to the root in our hearts. If we are regularly pursuing Christ through reading His Word and submitting our lives to Him, we will not be able to keep the goodness from flowing from our lips to others. Our eyes will see people with compassion, our minds will think of others with clarity and good reason, and our hearts will react to others with grace. However, if we are regularly pursuing the world through reading other people's opinions and submitting our lives to their standards of right and wrong, good and bad, we will not be able to keep the garbage from flowing out of our lips. Our eyes will see people with prejudices and biases, our minds will think of others with self-justified bitterness, and our hearts will react to others with revenge. You can't get apple juice from an orange, no matter how hard you squeeze it.

Scripture has so much to say about our tongues. In just one chapter of Proverbs, chapter 10, seven verses address the subject.

> The mouth of the righteous is a fountain of life, but the mouth of the wicked conceals violence. **Proverbs 10:11**

> Out of the lips of him who has understanding, wisdom is found. **Proverbs 10:13**

> The wise lay up knowledge, but the mouth of a fool brings ruin near. **Proverbs 10:14**

> The tongue of the righteous is choice silver; the heart of the wicked is of little worth. **Proverbs 10:20**

> The lips of the righteous feed many, but fools die for lack of sense. **Proverbs 10:21**

> The mouth of the righteous brings forth wisdom, but the perverse tongue will be cut off. **Proverbs 10:31**

> The lips of the righteous know what is acceptable, but the mouth of the wicked, what is perverse. **Proverbs 10:32**

---

[24] https://mississippimom.com/tame-your-tongue.

Our words matter. Our tone matters. Our intent matters. They all reveal what is inside. Pursue Christ, gain wisdom, and let Christ tame your tongue. Who else can tame it? James tells us who.

> No human being can tame the tongue. It is a restless evil, full of deadly poison. **James 3:8**

Our only hope for taming the tongue is giving Christ full reign of our hearts, minds, and mouths.

Change for Jesus

I bet someone wrote, "Never change!" or something like that in one of your yearbooks. I always thought that was such terrible advice. What if you had taken that advice seriously? What if you froze your development in whatever grade you received that magical advice? What if you lived like, spoke like, and fixed your hair like you did as a seventh grader? What if you never learned another thing past ninth grade? What if you kept the same part-time job and drove the same car you had in eleventh grade? What if you never grew up? What if you wore the same outfits? I realize that last question might have gone too far. Some of the men reading this feel targeted, and some of their wives feel vindicated. OK—you can keep the shirt you had in high school, but other things have to change. Change is necessary for health and life. When we have a heart of stubbornness and refuse to make necessary changes in our attitudes and actions, we might as well be driving that same car, headed to that same job, and wearing that same pair of boot-cut jeans.

If Jesus were signing your yearbook, He wouldn't write, "Never change." What would He write? Jesus calls us to change constantly. Maybe He would write something like what Paul told the church at Ephesus.

> Now this I say and testify in the Lord, that you must no longer walk as the Gentiles do, in the futility of their minds. They are darkened in their understanding, alienated from the life of God because of the ignorance that is in them, due to their hardness of heart. They have become callous and have given themselves up to sensuality, greedy to practice every kind of impurity. But that is not the way you learned Christ!— assuming that you have heard about him and were taught in him, as the truth is in Jesus, to put off your old self, which belongs to your former manner of life and is corrupt through deceitful desires, and to be renewed in the spirit of your minds, and to put on the new

self, created after the likeness of God in true righteousness and holiness. **Ephesians 4:17–24**

Notice Paul's clarification, "Assuming that you have heard about him and were taught in him, as the truth is in Jesus." We make a huge mistake when we think that going to church or even being a member of a church means we have "heard about Jesus and been taught in him." Just because someone sits in the room where the gospel is proclaimed doesn't mean they are hearing and learning.

The how-to is found at the end of this passage. Followers of Christ must put off their old self, which is corrupt, and put on the new self, which is righteousness. How? Authentic Christians imitate the likeness of God, and we have been introduced to the likeness of God in the God-man, Jesus. Model your life after the life of Jesus and anyone else you know who is rightly imitating Him. In Paul's words, "Be imitators of me, as I am of Christ" (1 Corinthians 11:1).

Give up Your Seat, Your Preferences, and Anything Else You Can if it Means Advancing the Gospel

The gospel is not about getting all we can get, rather, it is about giving all we can give. We are free to do this because, in Christ, we already have more than enough.

> So if there is any encouragement in Christ, any comfort from love, any participation in the Spirit, any affection and sympathy, complete my joy by being of the same mind, having the same love, being in full accord and of one mind. Do nothing from selfish ambition or conceit, but in humility count others more significant than yourselves. Let each of you look not only to his own interests, but also to the interests of others. Have this mind among yourselves, which is yours in Christ Jesus, who, though he was in the form of God, did not count equality with God a thing to be grasped, but emptied himself, by taking the form of a servant, being born in the likeness of men. And being found in human form, he humbled himself by becoming obedient to the point of death, even death on a cross. **Philippians 2:1–8**

Jesus gave all He could give. We have been urged to count others more significant than ourselves and to do nothing from selfish ambition or conceit. It is our joy and honor to give up our seat for a guest or even a brother or sister in Christ. Instead of getting to the service early to get an aisle seat, we should leave the aisle seats for those who come in late—especially if someone asks us to move over and make room.

If incorporating a different style of music than we are used to will reach more people for Jesus, we should joyfully sing with our brothers and sisters in Christ. No matter what style of music you prefer, there was a time and place where someone considered it ungodly. Are the lyrics grounded in the Word of God and solid theology? If so, why does it matter if it is sung with a full band or just a piano and organ? "Because that's what I like." Behold, the Wrastlin' Mullet in all of its glory.

We are to serve one another and consider others more important than ourselves. Every little (and I do mean little, because let's be honest, none of us have been asked to leave our perfect home in Heaven and come to Earth to be ridiculed, mocked, beaten, and crucified for the sin of humanity) sacrifice we make can be met cheerfully when we remind ourselves of what Christ has done for each of us. One thing that might help is to repeat in your mind, "Christ did more for me than I'm doing for them. I can do this little thing." Or when you find yourself tempted to be unkind or rude to someone who has been unkind or rude to you, you can repeat in your mind, "Christ died for this person. The least I can do is smile and be gracious in this moment. I can smile. I can be patient. I can be kind." If for no other reason, do it for Jesus. Each person is made in the image of God, and that means they are worthy of dignity and respect.

Let the wrastlers be the spectacle. Let's be servants. Let's follow the life-giving path Christ has laid out for us as directed in Scripture.

> I therefore, a prisoner for the Lord, urge you to walk in a manner worthy of the calling to which you have been called, with all humility and gentleness, with patience, bearing with one another in love, eager to maintain the unity of the Spirit in the bond of peace. **Ephesians 4:1–3**

Chapter Four: The Billy Ray Mullet

Introduction

There is little argument that the most famous mullet in history was brandished by Billy Ray Cyrus, the one-hit wonder of early 90s country music. Billy Ray will forever be remembered for three things: "Achy Breaky Heart," his famous/infamous daughter Miley Cyrus, and the mullet by which all other mullets must be judged.

Just as Billy Ray rocked the model mullet, country music epitomizes Mullet Theology. Consider these songs:

"Unanswered Prayers," Garth Brooks
"When I Get Where I'm Going," Brad Paisley and Dolly Parton
"Believe," Brooks and Dunn
"Jesus Take the Wheel," Carrie Underwood
"Changed," Rascal Flatts

What do these songs have in common? They carry on a long tradition in country music of writing and recording songs about God, Jesus, salvation, angels, prayer, the importance of church, and other biblical themes. Many of these are even sung in churches across the cultural South.

What else do these songs have in common? They are on albums with other songs that don't represent Jesus, the gospel, or biblical principles in any way. "Unanswered Prayers" is on the *No Fences* album right after "Friends in Low Places." "When I Get Where I'm Going" is song number fourteen on the album *Time Well Wasted*. That album includes a song simply titled "Alcohol," and a radio theater-style story titled "Cornography." They are both as far from being Christlike as they sound. "Believe" shares an album with "Whiskey Do My Talkin'." "Jesus Take the Wheel" was Carrie Underwood's second big hit. Her third big hit was "Before He Cheats." Let's just say that song doesn't exactly promote an Ephesians 5 view of marriage and relationships. Rascal Flatts, who sang "Changed," is the same group that first brought nudity to country music videos. The controversial video for their song "Melt" included both male and female nudity. Lead singer Joe Don Rooney describes the creative process for that video this way, "We just said, 'Let's make the best [expletive] sexy video we can.'"[25]

Work hard, play hard, and pray hard. That's how one author described the themes of country music.[26] The problem is that country music's playing often conflicts with its praying. I (Derek) grew up listening to preachers talk about straddling the fence. Perhaps you've heard the same illustration. Following Jesus is on one side of the fence, and following the Devil by enjoying the sins of the culture is on the other side of the fence. Straddling the fence is trying to keep a foot on both sides. Nothing represents the broken spiritual condition of the cultural South better than the straddle-the-fence philosophy expressed in country music. I can still hear those preachers warning us. "Just remember," they'd say, "straddling the fence won't work because the Devil owns the fence."

Mullet Description

The Billy Ray Mullet is the center of the Mullet Theology universe. It talks about Jesus so much that it can be difficult to see the wild backside. The Billy Ray Mullet keeps Jesus in the front by acknowledging God often, mentioning Jesus by name on a regular basis, claiming to be a follower of Jesus, sporting Jesus-themed merchandise, and having surface level conversations about biblical topics such as Heaven, hell, angels, prayer, sin, salvation, etc. When Billy Ray turns around, however, the Jesus in the front gives way to the party in the back. It's church on Sunday morning but party on Saturday night. It's compromising morally in every arena of life but dropping an extra twenty in the plate at church. It's living as though Jesus has nothing to say about everyday life but making sure to acknowledge the Man upstairs.

---

[25] https://countrynow.com/remember-when-rascal-flatts-caused-controversy-with-their-i-melt-video/.
[26] https://thereviewsarein.com/2015/01/02/take-me-to-church-country-music-plays-hard-prays-hard/.

Mullet Sightings

In 2012, Thomas Rhett stirred controversy with the song "Beer with Jesus." According to Rhett, he wrote the song "about the Jesus that I know, or I feel like I know."[27] There are two observations about this song and artist. First, Thomas Rhett's comments reveal the foundational problem with the Billy Ray Mullet. The Billy Ray Mullet **reshapes Christianity into a personalized version that parties with the crowd on Saturday night and goes to church with the congregation on Sunday morning.**

Second, Thomas Rhett was unfairly criticized. That's not because "Beer with Jesus" wasn't a song worthy of criticism. The criticism was unfair because he was singled out when country music does this all the time! In fact, the best way to find the Billy Ray Mullet is to observe it in its natural habitat—country music lyrics. Consider a few examples. To honor copyright restrictions, we can't reprint the lyrics here, but we encourage you to look them up as they are referenced and described.

"Buy Dirt" follows a classic country music pattern in which an older man passes on wisdom to a younger man. The song encourages young men to buy land, find a good wife, find a good job, pray, and give a little money to the church offering.[28]

It sounds like good advice. What could be wrong with that? It's subtle, but if you read the lyrics carefully you'll notice that **a relationship with God is important—just as important as finding the right person to marry, investing in real estate, finding the right job, and building a great family.** The Billy Ray Mullet has no problem with Jesus, church, or the Bible. They make perfect accessories to a good life.

"Red Dirt Road" is a coming-of-age song about experiences that took place with a girlfriend on a red dirt road. The song doesn't mention anything explicit because that's not country music's style. The tone of the song, however, communicates a generally rebellious teenage spirit. The teenagers sneak out of the house, hang out on the red dirt road, drink a little beer, develop questionable theology about the path

---

[27] https://www.rollingstone.com/music/music-country/inside-country-musics-conflicted-relationship-with-religion-226559/.
[28] Davie, Jordan, "Buy Dirt," Track 2, *Buy Dirt*, MCA Nashville Records, 2021.

to Heaven, and somehow find a personal relationship with Jesus.[29] Once again, **Jesus plays an accessory role to the good southern life**.

Other country artists have documented characteristics of a good southern life. "Little Big Town" described a normal southern weekend as playing poker on Saturday night and going to church on Sunday morning.[30] To be sure, poker can be played innocently and without gambling, but that's not what's happening in this song.

In "My List" Toby Keith describes the things that constitute the good southern life. The list includes raising hell and giving a little money to the church.[31] Another Toby Keith song, "God Love Her," further exemplifies the Billy Ray Mullet. It's a song about a rebellious seventeen-year-old in a relationship that her parents do not approve of. If you read the lyrics, you'll notice three things: 1) religious language, 2) the girl holds tight to her Bible, and 3) the boy and God both love her.[32]

The message is clear. This couple wants the listener to know they have not abandoned God or the Bible. They are just living out the good ol' southern lifestyle of rebellion and adultery while clinging to the Bible. And although the girl's parents don't approve, God understands.

Maybe you think I'm stretching the meaning of that particular song. Maybe I'm being a little too hard on country music. Well, Miranda Lambert removes all doubt in "Heart Like Mine." Lambert describes her heart as one that Jesus would understand and imagines she and Jesus would get along well. At the same time, she bemoans marriage, says drinking makes her stronger, and pictures Jesus toasting her with a drink when she makes it to Heaven.[33]

"Jesus drank wine" and "the Bible says 'take a little wine for your stomach'" are often quoted quips of the Billy Ray Mullet. In the Christian cultural South, Jesus drinking wine with low alcohol content, cut with water, in place of unreliable drinking water, at meals and in times of serious devotion and prayer (Last Supper) has become a

---

[29] Brooks, Kix and Ronnie Dunn, "Red Dirt Road," Track 5, *Red Dirt Road*, Arista Nashville, 2003, CD.
[30] Little Big Town, "Boondocks," Track 2, *The Road to Here*, Equity, 2005, CD.
[31] Keith, Toby, "My List," Track 11, *Pull My Chain*, DreamWorks Records, 2001, CD.
[32] Keith, Toby, "God Love Her," Track 3, *That Don't Make Me a Bad Guy*, Show Dog Nashville, 2008, CD.
[33] Lambert, Miranda, "Heart Like Mine," Track 12, *Revolution*, Columbia Nashville, 2009, CD.

license to guzzle hard liquor until you can't walk straight or stop yourself from going home with someone other than your spouse.

At the heart of the Billy Ray Mullet lies the idea that you can have Jesus without changing anything about your life—especially the aspects of your life that conform to southern cultural norms. Adding a little bit of Jesus to an otherwise ungodly life is not unique to the cultural South. What's unique is the attempt to integrate a little bit of Jesus into every part of life. That's why from one perspective, Christian culture is synonymous with southern culture. People in the cultural South assume they can keep Jesus in the front AND the party in the back. They assume they can live like hell and be part of the Kingdom of Heaven. Kenny Chesney and Joe Diffie have lyricized this belief.

In "Everybody Wants to Go to Heaven," Chesney recalls a conversation with a preacher. The preacher calls for right living, but Chesney informs the preacher he's too busy having fun for that right now. In fact, he's put $30 in the offering. According to the lyrics, that should pay for all his sins and leave enough to encourage the preacher to let God know, during his prayer time, that Chesney wants to go to Heaven—eventually—just not right now.[34]

Joe Diffie takes things a step farther. In "Prop Me Up Beside the Jukebox (If I Die)," Joe asks his friends to keep his body at the party as long as possible. He wants to go to heaven, but he doesn't want to go tonight. As his body occupies its spot at the jukebox, he wants a stiff drink and a blonde mannequin to keep him company. He wants to be the life of the party even when he's dead.[35]

How can Kenny and Joe's "I want to go to Heaven, just not right now" attitude ever be reconciled with this:

> For to me to live is Christ, and to die is gain . . . My desire is to depart and be with Christ, for that is far better.
> **Philippians 1:21, 23**

And how can anyone whose life is wrapped up in drinking and partying think they are part of the Kingdom of the Lord Jesus Christ?

I've spent most of my life in the cultural South, and I can testify that the Billy Ray Mullet doesn't stay locked away in country

---

[34] Chesney, Kenny, "Everybody Wants to Go to Heaven," Track 4, *Lucky Old Sun*, Blue Chair, 2008, CD.
[35] Diffie, Joe, "Prop Me Up Beside the Jukebox (If I Die)," Track 3, *Honkey Tonk Attitude*, Epic, 1993, CD.

music lyrics. It's woven into the fabric of the culture. People living in the cultural South know how to play church better than anyone on the planet. They know when to thank God for unanswered prayers and when to party with friends in low places. They know how to say they've given the wheel to Jesus while plotting revenge against an ex-boyfriend. They can tell the preacher how much they enjoyed the service—the same service during which they were texting with friends about the great party from the night before.

The most disturbing characteristic of the Billy Ray Mullet is that many people sitting in churches across the cultural South think it is supposed to be this way. It's just the southern way of life. They go to church, or at least they say they do; they believe in Jesus and the Bible, although they aren't really sure what the Bible says; they're for Christian morals unless those interfere too much with their lifestyles; they support conservative judges and Ten Commandments monuments, but just don't ask them to name the Ten Commandments; they're against communism, socialism, wokeism, and liberalism, but don't bother them with the details of biblical theology that counteract those *isms*.

In general, the Billy Ray Mullet doesn't think of being against anything Jesus is for or for anything Jesus is against. This mullet wants to keep things good with the Man upstairs. But it also doesn't want Him in the center of everything. The problem is that Jesus will only be part of your life if He can be Lord of your life.

Mullet Dangers

The greatest danger of the Billy Ray Mullet is that it promises salvation while leaving people dead in their trespasses and sins. Those who treat Jesus as just another part of a good southern life will be separated from God for all of eternity. For many people, part of life in the cultural South is raising a hand, walking an aisle, completing a card, attending a class, being baptized, or some other religious experience which we commonly refer to as "getting saved." When it comes time for funerals in the cultural South, everyone wants to know when the deceased "got saved." Friends and family will cling to almost any hint of a moment of salvation regardless of how little of an impact Jesus had on the deceased's life. Getting saved is part of the Jesus in the front section of the Billy Ray Mullet. The great danger lies in this—many salvation experiences people cling to do not match a biblical description of salvation.

I believe, without a doubt, "The vilest offender who truly believes that moment from Jesus a pardon receives."[37] A sinner can be saved in a moment. Churches should preach the gospel and call for a response. It doesn't matter if the response includes a raised hand, a completed card, a meeting with a pastor, or a walk down the aisle. But it must include true repentance and faith. If there is no repentance and faith, there is no salvation.

> Repent for the Kingdom of heaven is at hand. **Matthew 4:17**

> Unless you repent, you will all likewise perish. **Luke 13:3**

> Repentance for the forgiveness of sins should be proclaimed in his name to all nations. **Luke 24:47**

> If you confess with your mouth that Jesus is Lord and believe in your heart that God raised him from the dead, you will be saved. **Romans 10:9**

> For by grace you have been saved through faith. **Ephesians 2:8**

But salvation is not a one and done experience. It's not a rite of passage like getting your driver's license. Once you pass the driving test and get your driver's license, you have it for life. That is, of course, as long as you remember to renew it and you don't do something so serious that it gets taken away. That's how many people in the cultural South view salvation. They got saved when they were eight or ten or sixteen or twenty-six. Now that they have salvation, as long as they occasionally tip their hat to the Man upstairs and drop a little money in the plate at church, they can't lose it. That is, of course, unless they commit some really bad sin.

Salvation is not like that at all. It is true that Christians "get saved." That's called justification. It happens at the moment a person repents of sin and places their faith in Jesus. But Christians are also being saved. That's called sanctification.[38] It's an ongoing, day-by-day, step-by-step process through which God shapes the Christian more

---

[37] Crosby, Fanny J. "To God Be the Glory, Great Things He Hath Done," 1872.

[38] The terms justification, sanctification, and glorification are used by theologians to describe (respectively) the moment a believer first repents and is made right with God, the ongoing process of spiritual growth after salvation, and the process which takes place at death or the return of Christ through which all remaining sin is removed from the believer. While the Bible teaches all three concepts, it does not always use those terms in such tightly defined categories. Justification and sanctification are often used interchangeably in Scripture to speak of the moment of salvation.

into the image of Jesus. Romans 8:29 explains, "Those he foreknew he also predestined to be conformed to the image of his Son."

In Greek, the language of the New Testament, *sanctify* is the verb form of the word often translated "holy." To be sanctified is to be holied, or set apart as holy. Sometimes the word is translated as "saints." Who are the saints? They are the ones who have been holied or set apart. They are the set apart ones. In other words, if those who "get saved" are truly saved, they will continue the process of being saved after the moment of decision. They will grow in Christlikeness throughout the course of their lives and will look more and more like Jesus and less and less like the culture. Consider these verses:

> Therefore, if anyone is in Christ, he is a new creation. The old has passed away; behold, the new has come.
> **2 Corinthians 5:17**

> What shall we say then? Are we to continue in sin that grace may abound? By no means! How can we who died to sin still live in it? Do you not know that all of us who have been baptized into Christ Jesus were baptized into his death? We were buried therefore with him by baptism into death, in order that, just as Christ was raised from the dead by the glory of the Father, we too might walk in newness of life . . . We know that our old self was crucified with him in order that the body of sin might be brought to nothing, so that we would no longer be enslaved to sin. **Romans 6:1–4, 6**

> Put to death therefore what is earthly in you: sexual immorality, impurity, passion, evil desire, and covetousness, which is idolatry. On account of these the wrath of God is coming. In these you too once walked, when you were living in them. But now you must put them all away. **Colossians 3:5–8**

> For this is the will of God, your sanctification: that you abstain from sexual immorality; that each one of you know how to control his own body in holiness and honor, not in the passion of lust like the Gentiles who do not know God.
> **1 Thessalonians 4:3–5**

There are many more verses in the New Testament that give us the same message—those who are united to Christ through salvation will live obedient, godly lives. Not perfect lives, but godly lives. The Billy Ray Mullet rejects the idea that God demands obedience from those who follow Him. Jesus is in the front—He might be described or thought of as a best friend, a ride or die, or One who understands.

Whatever and Whoever Jesus is, He has no business changing the party in the back. After all, it's not about rules and regulations. It's about a relationship (for more on that, see the 'Dega Mullet). Jesus, however, defined the relationship in this way, "If you love me, you will keep my commandments" (John 14:15).

While it is true that the greatest danger of the Billy Ray Mullet is the false narrative presented about salvation, that's not the only danger. There aren't many things that cause more anxiety in southern church culture than rap music. And with good reason.[39] *Most* rap songs glorify sexual immorality, drug use, and violence, and that's just too much for the moral sensibilities of the Christian cultural South. Here's the deal—if you're going to write off rap music because of the immorality it glorifies, then to be consistent, you have to write off country music for the same reason. Rap music glorifies sexual immorality, drug use, and violence with expletive-laced rhymes; country music does it with a twang and a smile.

"But," someone might say, "they are just singing about life in the South." Rappers are just singing about life on the streets. "It's just entertainment. They don't actually live out those songs and neither do I," someone else might say. Nate Dogg and Warren G didn't actually "regulate"[40] anymore than Charlie Daniels ever took someone out to the swamp and left them for the alligators.[41]

Let me be clear—I'm not saying all country music is bad, and I'm not defending the kind of rap music that glorifies sin. I'm simply making a point. The Billy Ray Mullet is as blind to the sins of the cultural South as some folks are to the immorality of much of country music. Such blindness has a numbing effect. When we listen to songs that glorify the sins of our culture over and over again, we no longer see the sins of our culture. If we can't see the sins of our culture, it is only a matter of time before we come to regularly practice the sins of our culture.

Mullet Makeover: Christ-Centered Principles to Reshape Your Theology

---

[39] The style of music often referred to as rap is morally neutral. There are rap songs and rap artists who use the medium to communicate positive messages, God-honoring truth, and beauty. Some rap artists use the medium to present the gospel and teach biblical and theologically solid principles. Here "rap" refers to the most pervasive artists and songs of the rap genre.

[40] Griffin III, Warren, "Regulate," Track 1, *Regulate...G Funk Era*, 1997, CD.

[41] Daniels, Charlie, "Simple Man," Track 7, *Simple Man*, Epic, 1989, Cassette.

Take some time to tell your heart the truth, no matter how achey or breaky it might feel. This mullet just isn't working for you. It really has affected how you think, believe, and act. It's time to sober up and turn off the same ol' song you've been playing in your mind. Resist the urge to find your friends in low places. Instead, try tuning in to these Christ-centered principles.

Jesus on Saturday Night AND Sunday Morning

And Monday, and Tuesday, and Wednesday, and Thursday, and even Friday. Jesus is Lord, and we cannot compartmentalize His Lordship over our lives. That kind of compartmentalization doesn't work in other relationships. We can't say to our spouses, "Tomorrow morning, I'm all yours, but tonight I'm going on a date with someone else." What about the military? Try telling an enlistment officer, "I'm totally committed to being part of the US military one day per week, but the other six days, I'd like to have the freedom to work for the People's Republic of China."

In the same way, we can't serve Jesus as Lord on Sunday and indulge our sinful desires the rest of the week. Jesus said,

> No one can serve two masters, for either he will hate the one and love the other, or he will be devoted to the one and despise the other. **Matthew 6:24**

Don't read this and think, "I need to do a little better. I know I can't get rid of the small sins, but I really do need to eliminate the big sins and try to cut back on the medium sins." It doesn't work that way. When we come to Jesus, it's not to "do a little better." We come to Jesus to surrender. We lay down our weapons and throw up our hands. We give up complete control over our own lives and agree to do whatever He asks us to do. We're like the prodigal son of Luke 15 who rehearsed his speech to his father.

> I will arise and go to my father, and I will say to him, "Father, I have sinned against heaven and before you. I am no longer worthy to be called your son. Treat me as one of your hired servants." **Luke 15:18–19**

When we surrender to Jesus, we submit to His Lordship over our lives 24/7/365 plus leap year's extra day. He is Lord of all and Lord over all.

Party on Saturday Night AND Sunday Morning

But who wants to do that? You! At least you would if you knew where the real party is. The party, meaning the place where we find fellowship, fulfillment, and joy is not where the culture says it is. Frankly, you would be a fool to settle for the cheap experience the culture calls a "party." It will leave you feeling alone, empty, and nauseous.

God is not trying to pull you away from life. He's trying to bring you into a much better life. And I'm not just talking about Heaven. I'm talking about the Kingdom of God on earth. There is no place on earth where you will find more authentic friendship, deeper joy, more lasting fulfillment, and real life than you will find in Jesus. When we settle for the party on Saturday night, church on Sunday morning, straddle-the-fence, Jesus as an accessory kind of life, we miss out on the real thing. That's why Jesus said this:

> If anyone would come after me, let him deny himself and take up his cross and follow me. For whoever would save his life will lose it, but whoever loses his life for my sake and the gospel's will save it. **Mark 8:34–35**

Jesus doesn't call us to lay down our lives because He needs sacrifice. He calls us to lay down our lives because He, as our Creator, knows that is the only way we will find true life. It sounds like an oxymoron—die to live. But that is the path of following Jesus. Deny yourself. Take up your cross. Follow Jesus. Where did Jesus go when He took up His cross? To death. He calls us to follow Him to the cross. Paul described his relationship with Jesus this way:

> I have been crucified with Christ. It is no longer I who live, but Christ who lives in me. And the life I now live in the flesh I live by faith in the Son of God, who loved me and gave himself for me. **Galatians 2:20**

The path that Jesus lays out for us and the path that Paul followed is the path that leads to death—death to sin and self. That's where Jesus went when He took up His cross, and it's where He calls us to go as we follow Him. Don't forget, however, that death is not the end. The journey for Jesus did not end in death. That's why He adds the promise of life to the call to follow Him to death. If you will lay down your life for Jesus, He will give you new and abundant life. That was Paul's testimony as well. He didn't end with "I no longer live." He added, "The life I now live in the flesh, I live by faith in the Son of

God, who loved me and gave himself for me." It might sound like a contradiction, but through the power of the gospel, death leads to life.

When it comes to parties, Christian parties should be the best. We have more to celebrate than anyone else, and we have a family all over the world ready to join in the celebration. It really is remarkable. We can connect with one another in meaningful ways every day of the week, especially in worship on the Lord's Day.

We are also called to serve one another, to meet each other's physical, spiritual, and emotional needs. Many churches describe it as "living life together." The New Testament says it this way:

> Bear one another's burdens, and so fulfill the law of Christ. For if anyone thinks he is something, when he is nothing, he deceives himself. **Galatians 6:2–3**

> Love one another with brotherly affection. Outdo one another in showing honor ... Rejoice with those who rejoice, weep with those who weep. Live in harmony with one another.
> **Romans 12:10, 15–16**

Our gatherings are so great that we don't need alcohol to bring life to the party. The Holy Spirit does that. Real Christian fellowship and community is so kind, caring, and loving, that we don't need the fake and shallow friendships forged at weekend parties. Maybe you've had bad experiences with "church people" so you're inclined to think, "Those things sound good, but the church is full of hypocrites." And the clubs, bars, and parties are not? In some ways, it's true. We are all hypocrites. There are times when we all do or say things we pretend that we do not do or say. But when most people say that about church people, they are referring to totally fake people that bear no resemblance to Jesus. The church is not full of hypocrites. It is full of real, genuine people living for Jesus who are mixed in with others who are just faking it. Invest the time and relational work to identify who's who, and live your life in real Christian community.

Chapter Five: The Picture Day Mullet

Introduction

Some of the best mullets I (Lindsay) have seen are perfectly accented by colorful canvas backdrops and studio lighting. These mullets were captured on that most important day of the year—picture day. We all have memories of school picture days. Did you ever forget it was picture day only to regret your outfit and hair choices for decades? Or maybe you were one of those—you never forgot picture day. In fact, you laid out the clothes the night before, woke up early to fix your hair just right, and thinking, "I nailed it." Chances are that the best laid plans of outfit and hair have not stopped you from regretting the picture decades later.

Derek once planned what he thought was the perfect picture day. Like many boys in fourth grade, he was obsessed with all things military. Y'all, he and his brother had a legit Navy Seal handbook on self-defense which included multiple ways of "neutralizing" an enemy. But that's a topic for another book. Back to the story. He didn't lie to his parents. He just conveniently forgot to tell them picture day was coming. When the big day came, he was dressed in army fatigues complete with his "Allen" name patch. To make sure the look was complete, he snuck in a standard issue, Dessert Storm–era patrol cap and put it on for the picture. In case you're wondering, his mom was not happy about the picture, BUT, decades later, Derek does not regret it.

Here's the thing about picture day. It only captures a snapshot. We all hope the picture captures the best version of ourselves. The truth is a single, two-dimensional image cannot even come close to fully representing the person being photographed. On picture day, some mullets might easily be hidden if the hair was brushed back just right and the chin was tilted properly. A good photographer can take the picture in such a way that no one looking at the picture would even notice the mullet. The problem, though, is that the mullet is still there, and life isn't lived in a portrait studio.

Mullet Description

The Picture Day Mullet is all about keeping up appearances, putting your best face forward, presenting what you want others to see, and subtly hiding the truth. The Picture Day Mullet keeps Jesus in the front by looking good when the camera is on and saying the right things when someone is looking. The party in the back comes out when the picture we present to others is found to be as thin as a freshly trimmed wallet-sized photo from Olan Mills. In the cultural South, many people live like picture day is every day. They count on good lighting and careful editing to make sure no one sees the less than perfect truth.

Mullet Sightings

The Picture Day Mullet comes in various poses. A very common pose, let's call it Pose A, is the **"Here's a Casserole"** pose. Southerners often strike this pose when someone is going through a difficult time like sickness, loss of a loved one, or other devastating news. This seems to be a biblical response. After all, didn't Jesus say when we feed those who are hungry it's like we were feeding Him? Yes! He did![42] He also said to give water to the thirsty, invite strangers in, tend to the sick, clothe the naked, and visit the imprisoned.[43] The disconnect here is that many southerners hear of a brother or sister in Christ in deep despair and our initial, and sometimes only, response is to set up a meal train. I have personally benefited from multiple meal trains in my life, but I cannot say I have experienced just as many deep and authentic relationships with those who provided the meals. The relationship investment lasts about as long as the leftover chicken pot pie. It is as if some think they can cook their way out of bearing one another's burdens.

---

[42] Matthew 25:35
[43] Matthew 25:3140

Don't get me wrong, when a new mom is trying to nurse a crying baby, entertain a toddler, and avoid drowning in a sea of laundry, not having to cook dinner is a welcomed blessing. In other words, let's not stop the meal trains! But maybe it is time to move beyond the pretty dinner presentation and really get to know the mom on a deeper level. Maybe we could encourage the family with heartfelt prayers and encouragement. Maybe we could even ask specific questions that will allow and encourage the overworked mom to open up about her struggles. I've had a significant amount of experiences with such situations, and I can tell you, a little hand-written note with God's Word included can go a long way.

Pose B of the Picture Day Mullet package is the **"Bless Your Heart"** pose. When the untrained ear hears a southerner say this cute little phrase, it sounds sweet. On the contrary, it's as bitter as unsweet tea. They even usually have a sugary smile plastered on their face when they say it. If Google Translate had "southerner" as an option in its drop-down menu, this phrase would translate something like this, "Well . . . aren't you just so cute and stupid?"

To be fair, there are times when someone uses this phrase to mean, "I hate you are going through that." Only a well-trained southern ear can hear the difference. Even then, the Picture Day Mullet can rear its ugly backside. "Bless your heart" can be used somewhat sincerely to extend a surface level sympathy that is not moved to action. As Wikipedia states, "[Bless your heart] is primarily used by individuals who wish to "be sweet" and do not wish to "act ugly.""[44] I am pretty sure if Jesus was telling the parable of the Good Samaritan to cultural Christians, He would have included that the priest and Levite both whispered out a good "Bless your heart" to the beaten man in the ditch as they passed by.

Pose C of the Picture Day Mullet is one I almost overlooked. It's that pose you skim past because it's just blah. This one can be called the **"Sorry About the Mess"** pose. It took me leaving the cultural South and returning to even notice this little pose existed. A southerner will use the phrase, "Sorry about the mess" when a visitor enters their home, a passenger enters their car, or a guest stops by their office. The weird thing is that most of the time someone has told me this, I have noticed clear evidence of tidying up. It is a strange little mullet that likes to give the appearance of having everything in order most of the time, but this one time things just got a little out of place.

---

[44] https://en.wikipedia.org/wiki/Bless_your_heart.

Derek, my husband and co-author, admits that he sometimes wears this mullet. Derek functions best in an orderly environment, so he keeps his office well-organized. Except when he doesn't. On the occasions when his office is not exactly what he wishes it would be, he feels the need to apologize for "the mess," which, to most people, would really not be a mess at all. Derek explains it this way—he wants others to think of him as organized so he needs to apologize when even small areas seem out of order. Whatever you do, keep your eyes on the order in the front, and never look at that mess in the back!

During the seven years that we lived in Miami, Florida, I was invited to many homes, cars, and offices. No one ever told me, "Sorry about the mess," and plenty of them were messy. It was so refreshing to be welcomed into a not-so-perfect environment and know that what I saw was reality. I realized that I felt much more connected with the person because I had been invited into their reality. It revealed a part of my culture of origin I didn't know was there—the expectation of perfection. What a set up for failure!

The next pose of the Picture Day Mullet is like a value bundle. Pose D is the **"Jeremiah 29:11"** pose. I'm sure you know the reference.

> For I know the plans I have for you, declares the Lord, plans to prosper you and not to harm you, plans to give you hope and a future. **Jeremiah 29:11 NIV**

This pose captures the essence of all the bumper stickers and coffee cups from the crafty Christian store and sprinkles them as needed in life. Unfortunately, this pose of the Picture Day Mullet is a façade. It only includes the "pretty" parts of Scripture. It fails to read from the actual Bible to find out the full context of God's promise to the original audience. The people of Israel were being told that they would be in exile for seventy years before seeing a glimmer of this hopeful future. In fact, most of them would die in captivity. Cultural Christians like to crop the exile part out of the picture and get straight to the "hope and future" part. It doesn't look pretty in the frame, so they will just leave it out of the bundle.

Pose E of the Picture Day Mullet is **"Everything's All White (Right) on Easter."** This picturesque Mullet Theology says "Our Easter outfits are perfectly color coordinated, but our family is falling apart." This is fleshed out as family after family rides to churches all across the Bible Belt on any given Sunday, their minivan filled with conflict, selfishness, and greed. As soon as the tires find their stopping point in the church parking lot, the family steps out and turns into picture perfection. They are more concerned with the wrinkles the seatbelt created in their new suit than the relational damage caused by the argument during the car ride. What others see and perceive is most important.

The final pose of the Picture Day Mullet photo session is Pose F. It is actually a side-by-side collage of two related poses. It's the **"Y'all Come Back Real Soon"** pose alongside the **"Y'all Come Go With Us"** pose. It is one of the most famous portraits of the cultural South—the good ol' southern hospitality.

While it is absolutely true that southern hospitality is a beautiful aspect of southern culture and the rest of the country could use more of, it has its ugly side. As southerners, we are taught from childhood how to be the hostess with the mostest. We also learn and use polite voicing phrases of affection on a regular basis. We really do mean it when we say, "Y'all come back real soon." We hope they do! But when they do, we will be sure to spruce up our Picture Day Mullet, throw on our best complimenting outfit, fix our face, and stuff as much junk as we can in the closet as they are walking up the driveway.

Tidying up the house is more closely related to the "Sorry About the Mess" pose discussed above. But something else happens when we tidy up the house to impress people—we also hide all of our real issues. In the cultural South, we struggle to relax around friends, and we find it almost impossible to be authentic and vulnerable. It can take years, even decades, for southerners to show their real selves to someone.

In a previous book, *Trading Walls for Altars*, I (Lindsay) talk about the two walls we all have. Each of us has an inside wall and an outside wall. Those walls protect us from emotional harm, but they also prohibit us from experiencing real, healthy intimacy with those closest to us. In many cultures, the outside wall is high, but the inside wall is low. Those who have high outside walls don't seem friendly and welcoming. They seem rude and cold. That's not us. Southerners are world famous for friendliness and hospitality. We have low exterior walls. We might meet you on Sunday morning and have you over for dinner on Sunday night.

Cultures with high outside walls often have low outside walls. That's what we experienced when we served in Miami as church planting missionaries. Miamians have a reputation for being rude, but once you get past the thin, rude exterior, they will open up and share their lives with you. While southerners have low outside walls, our inside walls are a mile high and half a mile thick. We will invite you over for dinner after only knowing you for a brief moment (especially if you know a friend of a friend of a friend), but we are much less likely to share with each other our real fears, concerns, struggles, and failures.

Mullet Dangers

The Picture Day Mullet theology is harmful. It demonstrates the culturally Christian southerner's hesitation to be fully known by their brothers and sisters in Christ, which in turn diminishes the glory of God at work within their lives. Now, that doesn't mean the culturally Christian southerner doesn't want to fully know their brothers and sisters in Christ, or at least fully know their business. Cultural Christians are quick to listen to the juicy gossip about others, but slow to share their own struggles and personal victories Christ has won on their behalf.

Augustine warned of this unhealthy behavior.

> Men are a race curious to know of other men's lives, but slothful to correct their own. Why should they wish to hear from me what I am, when they do not wish to hear from You (God) what they are themselves?[45]

The Picture Day Mullet reveals something about us. We don't want to think about our own faults. It is just easier to pretend they don't exist. First Corinthians 10 reminds us that our relationships with one another are to be more than surface level politeness.

> The cup of blessing that we bless, is it not a participation in the blood of Christ? The bread that we break, is it not a participation in the body of Christ? **1 Corinthians 10:16**

Our fellowship with one another should move deeper than feel-good, empty conversations. Then, we can fully participate with one another in giving glory to God for doing what only He can do in bringing life to our death.

Jesus also warns of this kind of hypocrisy in Matthew 23. His description of the Pharisees bears some unsettling resemblances to the Picture Day Mullet.

---

[45] Augustine, *The Confessions,* Revised (Indianapolis, IN: Hackett Publishing Company, 2007), 190.

I would encourage you to read the chapter in full, but it comes to a head with this summary:

> Woe to you, scribes and Pharisees, hypocrites! For you are like whitewashed tombs, which outwardly appear beautiful, but within are full of dead people's bones and all uncleanness. So you also outwardly appear righteous to others, but within you are full of hypocrisy and lawlessness. **Matthew 23:27–28**

Mullet Makeover: Christ-Centered Principles to Reshape Your Theology

So you've seen the photo proofs from picture day, and it's not really a picture you want hanging on the wall of your parent's house for the next few decades. You've seen the Picture Day Mullet and realized it ain't pretty. It's time to trim that mullet and get a respectable hairstyle. How can we breathe life into our whitewashed tombs of death? We can't. Only Jesus can! Here are four Christ-centered principles that can reshape that Picture Day Mullet into biblical authenticity and fill your emptiness with life.

Biblical Community Instead of Christian Cliques

God created us to live in community with one another. The cultural Christian version of community is the "us four and no more" mentality. We have a few relationships we are comfortable with, and everyone else is an outsider. The problem with that mentality is that Scripture describes the church in this way:

> So we, though many, are one body in Christ, and individually members one of another. **Romans 12:5**

We are connected to a large group of people. Paul even uses the word, "many." The human body is full of many intricate parts that need one another in order to function properly. So, too, is the body of Christ. We function best when we live in authentic community with one another.

How do we cultivate biblical community? Peter gives us five practical ways we can function properly as the family of God.

> Finally, all of you, have unity of mind, sympathy, brotherly love, a tender heart, and a humble mind. **1 Peter 3:8**

51

First, Peter calls us to unity of mind. Unity is more than simple union (just being together) and less than uniformity (being identical). It means being like-minded even when we don't share exactly the same thoughts. It means doing the hard work of thinking deeply about our beliefs and convictions as a group. As God's people, using Scripture as our source of knowledge and wisdom, we can sit with Bibles open and hearts tuned to one another until there is unity of mind.

Second, Peter calls us to sympathy. When we are moved to tears—and even better, to action—on behalf of our brother or sister, we display true compassion and sympathy for them. We get into the fight with them, and we feel their pain. We bear their burdens.

Third, Peter calls us to brotherly love. We are not just friends, acquaintances, or neighbors. We are family. We share a Father and an inheritance, and we have been bought with the same blood. Perhaps you haven't thought much about this, but we will be spending eternity with one another. God calls us to live in true community with other believers here so that we are prepared to live in eternal community hereafter.

Fourth, Peter calls us to have a tender heart. This is something Paul also commands us to pursue. He says it this way:

> Be kind to one another, tenderhearted, forgiving one another, as God in Christ forgave you. **Ephesians 4:32**

What is the key to tenderheartedness according to this passage? When we realize how greatly God in Christ has forgiven us, we can forgive one another. Seeing others through the lens of grace leads to tenderheartedness and kindness (more on kindness in a moment).

Fifth, Peter calls us to have a humble mind. Community with others is deepened when the members of the community are humble and teachable. When we take a "me first" or "my way or the highway" approach to life, we act like the wrong end of a magnet. We push away what we should be attracting.

These compelling characteristics of biblical community are richer, deeper, and longer lasting than those of the shallow counterpart that many of our southern friends live in. When you find yourself isolating from others and lacking authentic relationships with God's people, choose to press in toward biblical community instead. Love God AND His people. Love them not because they are pretty, fun, and loveable. Love them because Christ loves them (and you) and gave

Himself up for them (and you) while they (and you) were still sinners (paraphrase of Romans 5:8).

> We love because He first loved us. **1 John 4:19**

> A new commandment I give to you, that you love one another: just as I have loved you, you also are to love one another. By this all people will know that you are my disciples, if you have love for one another. **John 13:34–35**

What does it look like to love one another as He has loved us? It looks like us giving up our lives for one another. That's what Jesus did. That's what He has called us to do.

Biblical Kindness Instead of Southern Politeness

There is a difference between kindness and politeness, as evidenced in the "Bless Your Heart" pose. During a recent visit to Southeast Asia, we noticed some cultural similarities between Indonesians and southerners. They were very polite and wouldn't dream of saying anything harsh. That didn't necessarily mean they were always being kind.

One day, we met an elderly farmer in a village and began to have a conversation with him. Derek, planning to share the parable of the sower, asked him if he could tell him a farming story from the teachings of Jesus. Everything changed. Our tour guide, who was not a believer, said, "Oh, the old men in this village are all hard of hearing. I don't think he will be able to hear or understand your story. We should just go on." Funny, he seemed to be hearing just fine up to that point. The men would never just come out and say, "We don't believe that, and we don't want to hear about it."

What is the difference between kindness and politeness? Politeness is not a bad thing, but without kindness, it's empty. Good manners are a big deal in the South. Saying "yes, ma'am, no, sir, please, and thank you" are highly valued, but unfortunately true kindness can be hard to find. Consider some of the biblical marks of kindness. In 2 Timothy, Paul encourages Timothy to be kind even when correcting his opponents.

> And the Lord's servant must not be quarrelsome but kind to everyone, able to teach, patiently enduring evil, correcting his opponents with gentleness. **2 Timothy 2:24–25**

That means kindness is more than simply saying polite words. The Cambridge Dictionary definition of polite uses this sentence as an example of the word: "He was too polite to point out my mistake."[46] Kindness, according to Paul, can include pointing out mistakes and even correcting people who are your opponents.

> In Colossians 3, Paul provides more details about kindness.

> Put on then, as God's chosen ones, holy and beloved, compassionate hearts, kindness, humility, meekness, and patience, bearing with one another and, if one has a complaint against another, forgiving each other; as the Lord has forgiven you, so you also must forgive. **Colossians 3:12–13**

Did you see a common thread? Both verses speak of patience, getting along, and meekness or gentleness. The Colossians passage gives us a little more detail in how—through mutual forgiveness. When we are people of patience, peacemaking, and meekness, we are people of kindness.

Biblical Confession Instead of Hypocrisy and Hiding

So what hope is there for families who try Sunday after Sunday to straighten all the wrinkles as they walk from the parking lot to the pew? How do we fight the urge to wear the Picture Day Mullet every single Sunday and all the days in between? We fight against one of the enemy's biggest lies—as long as no one knows, everything will be OK, and no one will get hurt.

James contradicts that lie and commands us to pursue a path that leads to healing.

> Therefore, confess your sins to **one another** and pray for **one another**, that you *(y'all)* may be healed. The prayer of a righteous person has great power as it is working. **James 5:16** (emphasis added)

We have a listening part, a telling part, and a praying part to play in the healing work of the saints. The listening comes relatively easily, the telling and praying parts, not so much.

---

[46] https://dictionary.cambridge.org/us/dictionary/english/polite

Cultural Christians are hypocrites in the truest sense of the word. R. C. Sproul pushes back against the idea that Christians are all hypocrites.

> Though no Christian achieves the full measure of sanctification in this life, that we all struggle with ongoing sin does not justly yield the verdict of hypocrisy. A hypocrite is someone who does things he claims he does not do. Outside observers of the Christian church see people who profess to be Christians and observe that they sin. Since they see sin in the lives of Christians, they rush to the judgment that therefore these people are hypocrites. If a person claims to be without sin and then demonstrates sin, surely that person is a hypocrite. But for a Christian simply to demonstrate that he is a sinner does not convict him of hypocrisy.[47]

The step that makes us hypocritical is claiming to have it all together. That's the lie of the Picture Day Mullet. Authentic Christians know they are sinners and rejoice daily in the truth that they are saved by God's grace. In response to the objection that the church is filled with hypocrites, Dr. D. James Kennedy winsomely replied, "There's always room for one more."[48] The heart behind his answer gently reveals his awareness of his own sin. The church is a place where brothers and sisters marred by sin can join together and bring healing to one another. That healing can't happen if we aren't honest about our sin.

Biblical Hospitality Instead of Southern Hospitality

Biblical hospitality is all the good of southern hospitality without any of the bad. Southern hospitality will hold the door open for you, greet you with a warm smile and kind words, but return to gossiping about you once you're inside. Biblical hospitality, on the other hand, is an act of genuine love.

> Let love be genuine. Abhor what is evil; hold fast to what is good. Love one another with brotherly affection. Outdo one another in showing honor. Do not be slothful in zeal, be fervent in spirit, serve the Lord. Rejoice in hope, be patient in tribulation, be constant in prayer. Contribute to the needs of the saints and seek to show hospitality. **Romans 12: 9–13**

---

[47] https://www.ligonier.org/learn/articles/church-full-hypocrites.
[48] ibid

Biblical hospitality is so much more than just being nice. This is tough stuff. Abhor evil things, hold fast to good things, show affection for one another, show honor, constantly pray, serve together, rejoice together, be patient together, contribute to one another's needs. If our interactions with other believers looked more like this, our relationships would be so much deeper and more fulfilling.

So, get rid of that Picture Day Mullet and embrace the more authentic, clean-cut look: biblical community, biblical kindness, biblical confession, and biblical hospitality. It will look much better on you, and I promise you won't regret it decades from now.

Chapter Six: The Slater Mullet

Introduction

If you grew up in the 90s, *Saved by the Bell* was probably part of your life. The two male lead characters were Zack Morris and A. C. Slater. Zack was the cool "man with the plan." Slater was the school's sports star. Both guys were known for their hair. Zack's hair always seemed to be perfect, and Slater rocked an iconic curly mullet. In case you wanted to know, you can buy your very own Zack Morris or A. C. Slater wig on Amazon.

There was much more than hair to *Saved by the Bell*. If you look past the mullet (and the cheesy plot lines), it's clear that *Saved by the Bell* represented all the cultural norms of dating and relationships. Those norms are even apparent in the early years when the characters were in middle school. Unfortunately, much of the ideas about dating and relationships from pop culture have sneaked their way into the church as smoothly as Slater and Zack could sneak out of detention. Those unhealthy and unbiblical ideas have wreaked havoc on our marriages, our families, and our communities.

Mullet Description

The Slater Mullet puts Jesus in the front by keeping a few "nonnegotiables" when it comes to dating and sex. The party in the back, however, ignores true biblical purity. The Slater Mullet lies to its wearers by saying, "As long as you don't do these certain things, you're OK." It fails to address motives, thoughts, hearts, and the positive characteristics of godly relationships. It is a "thou shalt not" approach to dating, sex, and marriage rather than a "thou shall." Slater's mullet was always well kept, not too crazy in the back, and filled with plenty of hair product to make sure his curls stayed just where they should. It wasn't one of those out-of-control mullets you might see at the county fair. It was a well-kept mullet. What could go wrong with that? It turns out the Slater Mullet can make a big mess.

Mullet Sightings

Sadly, the Slater Mullet shows up most when adults discuss dating and relationship norms with the younger generation. In many cases, the theology of dating and relationships prevalent in the church has been shaped more by Bayside High than the Bible. Here are a few phrases I (Lindsay) have heard firsthand from cultural Christians.

"Boys will be boys," meaning, "boys are going to lust after young women and say and do things they shouldn't. There's nothing we can do to stop it, so why try?" This phrase carries a sense of hopelessness and wishful thinking that surely one day they will just grow out of it. A similar phrase I've often heard is **"You've gotta sow your wild oats."** The error of this statement should be so obvious, and I am doing all I can to hold back the biblical response until the proper section of this chapter. Many of these mullets would be easily avoided by just knowing and living by some basic truths taught in Scripture. We aren't talking about secret mysteries encoded so deeply in the original languages of the Bible that only a scholar can understand them.

You've probably looked at a mullet and thought, if I had a pair of scissors and that person would let me, I could just make a few quick snips and it would all be better! That's the way I feel about some of these phrases. They are so obviously unbiblical. I just want to get the scissors out and start cutting. But first, a few more common phrases.

Speaking to a child, "Do you have a boyfriend/girlfriend?" This phrase reveals a distorted view of the purpose for dating relationships. Dating or courtship is meant to be a preparation for marriage. A boyfriend or girlfriend is the title given to the person in a dating relationship. Why in the world would a child be in a dating relationship? A child is not anywhere near ready to prepare for marriage. It makes no sense! But I cannot count the times in a cultural Christian setting that I have heard this kind of language being used with small children. What are we teaching them when we say things like this? It sounds to me like we are teaching that romantic relationships can and should begin in preschool.

In her book, *Sex, Jesus, and the Conversations the Church Forgot,* Mo Isom charges the church by saying:

> Do we truly love another if we aren't helping to guard their heart, their body, and their spirit in purity and in obedience?[49]

She is speaking about your personal responsibility not to tempt others away from purity, but it also applies to how you encourage them with your speech away from patterns of purity.

I need to warn you, the next two phrases are disturbing on multiple levels. I want to be clear—these are things I have heard firsthand from southern people claiming to be Christians. Derek has heard them as well. The first was said by a mom to her teenage daughter when giving her advice about sex. **"Don't date a black boy or come home pregnant."** What?! How can that be considered remotely biblical? First, the Bible never condemns interracial marriage. If that comes as a shock to you, do your own research. Second, "don't come home pregnant" sets a really low bar for sexual purity. Without going into unnecessary detail, there are multiple acts that are sexually impure according to biblical standards that won't result in pregnancy. It also communicates that sexual intercourse is fine as long as it includes proper birth control methods. It further communicates that young women who do get pregnant shouldn't bother to come home. Or maybe there's hope if the young woman hides the pregnancy long enough to get an abortion.

The other disturbing phrase has been said by more than one father about a promiscuous college-aged son, **"At least my boy ain't gay."** These statements reveal such deep misunderstandings of sexual sin and the death it causes. The Jesus in the front of this mullet says, "We have standards that we are not willing to budge on when it comes to sex." Unfortunately, the party in the back sends the message that those standards have been set by the culture around them, not by the God of the Bible.

This last set of phrases are usually said lightheartedly, but behind every bit of sarcasm there lies some sincerity. Sadly these phrases are often said in front of the children they are talking about. In speaking about a beautiful young girl, **"Hope you have your shotgun ready, Dad."** This saying implies that the dad needs to be ready to shoot all the suitors who will be coming to date his daughter because she's so pretty. Next, in speaking of a handsome young boy, some say,

---

[49] Mo Isom, *Sex, Jesus, and the Conversations the Church Forgot* (Grand Rapids, MI: Baker Books, 2018), 141.

"That one's gonna be a lady killer!" I know it seems like I'm picking on a harmless quip meant to compliment a young man's good looks. But is it harmless for a good-looking guy to pass girls around and break their hearts until one day settling down and sticking with one lucky lady? We can do better. If we will think about what we are saying before we repeat these southern culture cliches, we will realize they are far from clean-cut. They are part of a mullet—the Slater Mullet.

Mullet Dangers

I hope you recognize some of the dangers of the Slater Mullet right away. This mullet is all about phrases adults in the church say to or about the younger generation in reference to sex, dating, and romantic relationships. I can just hear some people now in reaction to this chapter, "Lighten up, Lindsay. It's not that big of a deal!" Scripture says it is.

> Out of the abundance of the heart the mouth speaks... I tell you, on the day of judgment people will give account for every careless word they speak, for by your words you will be justified, and by your words you will be condemned.
> **Matthew 12:34, 36–37**

Those are pretty heavy words! What you say matters. What you mean by what you say matters. What children hear you say about them matters. In an article published by Desiring God, author Jon Bloom writes:

> The point is clear: words under control can do great good. They can be for others "a tree of life" (Proverbs 15:4) and "give grace to those who hear" (Ephesians 4:29). But uncontrolled, foolish words can burn friendships, families, churches, and careers to the ground (James 3:9–10).[50]

Foolish phrases of the Slater Mullet have done their part in producing a confused and distorted view of sexuality among culturally Christian teens. Purity is nowhere on the radar for most young people even within the church. They feel cultural pressures from outside the church and apathy or even banter from within the church that leads them to have romantic relationships and act on physical desires in a way that is so far from God's design.

---

[50] https://www.desiringgod.org/articles/our-tongues-and-fingers-of-fire.

Mullet Makeover: Christ-Centered Principles to Reshape Your Theology

Maybe you've started to notice that the Slater Mullet is not so cute after all. It's time for a trim. Commit these three Christ-centered principles to your heart. Your words will follow your heart. You will also reshape your theology (and the theology of your children) to be a theology that promotes purity instead of flirting with sexual immortality.

Sow Life Rather Than Death

You have likely heard the phrase "you reap what you sow." It seems common sense, but it is actually found in Scripture. Paul puts it this way:

> Do not be deceived: God is not mocked, for whatever one sows, that will he also reap. **Galatians 6:7**

This passage ties our actions to their consequences. It also reminds us that God will not allow our actions to mock Him. What He says leads to life *really* does lead to life, and what He says leads to death *really* does lead to death. We cannot sow seeds of death over and over again and wake up one day scratching our heads because the harvest looks and smells like death. Why would we encourage our children, or anyone for that matter, to "sow wild oats" and expect them to end up with anything other than wild results? Another common phrase of cultural Christianity is, "I don't know why they are living that way now. I raised them in church." For more on that, see the Joe Dirt Mullet. For now, just know it's not enough to just "raise them in church." You have a direct responsibility to teach your children how to honor God with their hearts, minds, and bodies.

Godly Counsel Rather Than Good Ol' Boy Counsel

You, parents, are responsible for teaching your child the biblical truth about sex. Yes, the church can help, but assuming the church is responsible for discipling your children is like assuming the dentist is responsible for making sure they brush their teeth. The church is called to support and provide resources to you as the primary discipler of your children. It is not capable of personally discipling each child. That task was given to the family (Proverbs 22:15).

It would take a separate book (or two) to give you more specifics on what this practically looks like. Thankfully two great resources have already been written! I can't say enough amazing things about the book *Mama Bear Apologetics: Empowering Your Kids to Understand and Live Out God's Design* and its counterpart, *Mama Bear Apologetics: Guide to Sexuality*. Both books offer shocking information and statistics, deep biblical truth, practical everyday applications, and abundant (free!) parental resources to help parents provide godly counsel to their children.

Your kids don't need another good ol' boy patting them on the back after their first date with a girl. They don't need to hear what sixteen-year-old you would have done in their shoes. They need to hear what God says about sex. I love how Desiring God's website worded it.

> God created sex. Because of our sin, sex often serves as part of our self-destruction. But God offers great hope of redemption, restoration, and real joy.[51]

They offer over 170 resources on the topic of sexual purity alone, including sermons, articles, podcasts, and FAQs.

Another aspect of godly counsel that the American church has largely abandoned is our role as parents in big decisions. That includes the decision about who our children will marry. We have bought the Hollywood lie that marriage is the individual's decision alone based on their feelings. According to this lie, parents have no part in the process. How sad. Our godly counsel as parents to our children has been silenced by our culture just when they need it most. We cannot take the "they'll figure it out" approach any longer. It begins with modeling a healthy marriage for them in their childhood, continues with helping them learn and understand God's design for relationships in the pressure cooker of puberty, and extends with biblical guidance as they consider dating, courting, and/or marriage as young adults.

While we are not proponents of arranged marriage, it is worth considering that modern western culture is the only culture in human history that does not practice some degree of arranged marriage. We assume our way is the only right way. But "our way" completely excludes parents from the dating and marriage decision-making process. That simply doesn't match the biblical pattern.

---

[51] desiringgod.org/topics/sexual-purity.

Careful Words Rather Than Careless Words

The book of Proverbs warns,

> Death and life are in the power of the tongue. **Proverbs 18:21**

Choosing to give life with your words can only happen when you have life at the source of your words . . . your heart. Jesus said it this way:

> The good person out of the good treasure of his heart produces good, and the evil person out of his evil treasure produces evil, for out of the abundance of the heart his mouth speaks. **Luke 6:45**

If you find that your words are not wholesome, well . . . time for a heart check. King David knew what it was like to have a heart in desperate need of cleaning. In his lament over the sin of adultery with Bathsheba he cried out to the Lord,

> Create in me a clean heart, O God, and renew a right spirit within me. **Psalm 51:10**

Our only hope for a clean heart is submitting ourselves to the Lord through confession, repentance, and acceptance of His forgiveness.

Careless words can reveal transgression (Proverbs 10:19); they are out of place in God's kingdom (Ephesians 5:4); they can cause mass destruction (James 3:1–18); they are an abomination to the Lord (Proverbs 12:22); and they can condemn you (Matthew 12:37).

> The heart of the righteous ponders how to answer, but the mouth of the wicked pours out evil things. **Proverbs 15:28**

Weigh your words carefully, don't just let them gush evil.

Take the first step to clean up your heart, your mind, and your mouth. Slip away from the Slater Mullet that promises pleasure but actually delivers emptiness and pain. Embrace the life found in biblical principles of purity, and believe Him when God says He knows the path to life (Psalm 16:11; Proverbs 15:24; Acts 2:28; John 14:6).

Chapter Seven: The 'Dega Mullet

Introduction

There's no better way to introduce this mullet than a (filtered) transcript of Ricky Bobby's prayer in the movie *Talladega Nights*.

Carley: Supper's ready! C'mon y'all. I've been slaving over this for hours.

Ricky: Dear Lord Baby Jesus, or as our brothers to the south call you, Jesús, we thank you so much for this bountiful harvest of Domino's, KFC, and the always delicious Taco Bell. I just want to take time to say thank you for my family, my two beautiful, beautiful, handsome, striking sons, Walker and Texas Ranger, or T.R. as we call him, and of course, my red-hot smoking wife, Carley who is a stone-cold fox. Who, if you were to rate her one to a hundred, it would easily be a ninety-four. Also wanna thank you for my best friend and teammate, Cal Naughton Jr. who's got my back no matter what.

Cal: Shake and Bake.

Ricky: Dear Lord Baby Jesus, we also thank you for my wife's father, Chip. We hope that you can use your Baby Jesus powers to heal him and his horrible leg. And it smells terrible and the dogs are always bothering with it. Dear tiny, infant Jesus, we . . .

Carley: Hey, you know, sweetie, Jesus did grow up. You don't always have to call him "baby." It's a bit odd and off-putting to pray to a baby.

Ricky: Well, I like the Christmas Jesus best and I'm saying grace. When you say grace you can say it to grown-up Jesus, or teenage Jesus, or bearded Jesus or whoever you want.

Carley: You know what I want? I want you to do this grace good so that God will let us win tomorrow.

Ricky: Dear tiny Jesus, in your golden-fleece diapers, with your tiny, little, fat, balled-up fists . . .

Chip: He was a man! He had a beard!

Ricky: Look, I like the baby version the best, do you hear me? I win the races and I get the money.

Cal: I like to picture Jesus in a tuxedo T-shirt, cause it says, like, "I wanna be formal, but I'm here to party, too." Cause I like to party, so I like my Jesus to party.

Walker: I like to picture Jesus as a ninja fighting off evil samurai.

Cal: I like to think of Jesus, like, with giant eagle's wings. And singing lead vocals for Lynyrd Skynyrd, with, like, a angel band. And I'm in the front row, and I'm hammered drunk.

Carley: Hey Cal, why don't you just shut up?

Cal: Yes, ma'am.

Ricky: Okay. Dear eight pound, six ounce newborn infant Jesus, don't even know a word yet, just a little infant and so cuddly, but still omnipotent, we just thank you for all the races I've won and the 21.2 million dollars—woo! (the rest of the family says "woo" too)—love that money that I have accrued over this past season. Also, due to a binding endorsement contract that stipulates I mention Powerade at each grace, I just want to say that Powerade is delicious and it cools you off on a hot summer day. And we look forward to Powerade's release of Mystic Mountain Blueberry. Thank you for all your power and your grace, dear baby God. Amen.[52]

---

[52] *Talladega Nights: The Ballad of Ricky Bobby*, Columbia Pictures, 2006.

Mullet Description

Like Ricky Bobby's prayer in *Talladega Nights*, the 'Dega Mullett reshapes Jesus to be whoever or whatever the individual wants Him to be at any given moment. The 'Dega Mullet keeps Jesus in the front by talking about Jesus often and even praying to Jesus. It keeps the party in the back by making Jesus out to be someone who wouldn't change anything about us or challenge us to do hard things. The 'Dega Mullet believes Jesus is just here to help us achieve our goals in life. He is only here to help us live our best life now.

Mullet Sightings

The 'Dega Mullet is not just found at the race track. Oh no. It travels. That hideous mullet pulls right into the back of the trailer and hauls itself all over the South (and beyond). You might recognize a few of its sponsored slogans.

I Want Jesus, Not Theology

The fine print of this slogan is "I just want the Jesus I have created in my head. I don't want to know the real Jesus or obey His commands. After all, He said that if I love Him, that's all that matters." The same Jesus Who said there was no commandment greater than loving God and loving others also said,

> If you keep my commandments, you will abide in my love, just as I have kept my Father's commandments and abide in his love. **John 15:10**

Jesus calls us to obey His commandments in the same way He obeyed the Father's commandments. If we do not know theology, how will we even know what His commandments are?

We tend to think of the Old Testament as the book of commands and the New Testament as the book of "just love Jesus and others." Around the time of Jesus, Jewish Rabbis had identified 613 commandments in the Old Testament.[53] According to some counts, the New Testament, which is much shorter than the Old Testament, contains 1050 commandments.

---

[53] The first historical reference to 613 commandments is from the third century BC. It is likely that this list existed much earlier, and it is highly possible that it was in use at the time of Jesus.

The truth is you have theology. Everyone does. Most people just have weak or bad theology. Jesus is the sum total, the pinnacle, the cornerstone, and the capstone of every ounce of solid theology. The better theology you have, the more Jesus you have.

There's a difference between knowing theological facts and having good theology. You can have a PhD in theology and have less real, true theological knowledge than a stay-at-home mom with only a high school education who spends time in the Word each day. One key to growing in true, biblical theology is obedience. When we obey and live out what we already understand, God reveals more of Himself to us.

Baby Jesus Is My Favorite Jesus

This little slogan sounds nice, but can you imagine standing face to face in front of the Creator, Redeemer, Mighty God, King of Kings, Alpha and Omega, High Priest, Master, Savior, and Judge (just to name a few) and quipping, "Well, aren't you just so cute?!" Can you fathom speaking to the Lion of the tribe of Judah like a little lap dog? This phrase connotes that Jesus is small and adorable but can leave the grown-up things to the real person in charge . . . you.

It's Not a Religion, It's a Relationship

This is a slogan that gets a lot of airtime in the South. For those who are forty and over, it is probably a helpful slogan. We grew up in an era when hyper-legalism could be found in many southern churches. Legalism simply means trying to work your way to God by following a list of dos and don'ts rather than relying on what Jesus has done for us. Many southern churches have struggled to flesh out the relationship between faith and works over the years, and sometimes faithful church attendance, Sunday school involvement, and giving have been emphasized more than a relationship with God. "It's not a religion, it's a relationship" began to remind believers that Christianity is a relationship with God which leads to good works, not the other way around.

As slogans often do, this slogan has come to mean something different in the twenty-first century. It has morphed into something much more mullet-like. The Jesus in the front is the emphasis on a relationship with God, but the party in the back is a complete disregard for following the commands of Jesus. "It's not a religion, it's a relationship" has come to mean "Me and Jesus are tight, so I don't need to go to church, live missionally, disciple my family, give, or practice any other spiritual disciplines."

For some Christians, "It's not a religion, it's a relationship" is something like a dating relationship. It's a dating relationship in which the couple goes out on the weekends, never sees each other throughout the week, doesn't take steps toward marriage, and tells everyone, "It's not about marriage, it's about the relationship." Sadly, and not coincidentally, that kind of dating relationship is becoming more popular as well. Because of the deep relationship we shared, Derek and I conducted a wedding ceremony where we dressed in special clothing, recited vows to one another, exchanged rings that would serve as symbols of our commitment each day we wore them afterward, gathered with others to commemorate the occasion, signed formal and legally binding documents, and I even changed my name. Our marriage is more than just a relationship. It's . . . well, it's a marriage.

I'm Fueled by Sweet Tea and Jesus

This slogan can be found on T-shirts, mason jars, and kitchen towels all over the cultural South. Let me translate what this version of the 'Dega Mullet is really telling you. "I'm gonna drink sweet tea every chance I can get. If the Milo's jug is running low in the refrigerator, I'll probably panic! Oh, and I like a little Jesus on the side when possible." Now, this mullet unapologetically complains when a restaurant only serves unsweet tea (or even worse, raspberry tea), but shrugs it off as no big deal when the TV evangelist or influential pastor makes a mockery of Jesus by preaching self instead of Savior. This mullet rarely entertains conversations about biblical things outside of a church setting or churched audience. Essentially, it is the Jesus + something-else kind of mentality. Jesus alone is not enough to make it through the day. I need something else.

Mullet Dangers

These 'Dega Mullet ideas demonstrate a lack of awe for the work and person of Jesus Christ. They downplay the importance of wisdom and knowledge, and diminish the glory of God. The slogans themselves are not the primary danger. We are sure there are plenty of people who faithfully follow Jesus and enjoy sweet tea on a regular basis. We're also sure there are many pastors who say "It's not a religion, it's a relationship" to help their congregations focus more on personal intimacy with God. The problem is that these cute little slogans have grown a big mullet. The slogans become the theology; they become the practice of Christians. The 'Dega Mullet has helped shape a religious philosophy in the cultural South which has diminished the seriousness of the gospel.

The 'Dega Mullet has also blunted the edge of real discipleship. Following Jesus is challenging. It requires all we have and all we are. With such cute mullets running around our churches, it's no wonder many husbands and fathers have checked out of church. We don't know who came up with the phrase, "I'm fueled by sweet tea and Jesus," but it wasn't a man. Men are not drawn to easy-believism, cheap grace, and cute phrases fit for a nice canvas print. For more on the absence of men in church, see the Joe Dirt Mullet.

The 'Dega Mullet has led to superficial bumper-sticker theologies which leave spiritual gas tanks empty. Our churches then become a collection of theological wreckage. If you want Jesus without all of the theology, you'll eventually lose Jesus. That creates a pile of wreckage with unfathomable consequences.

We have a discipleship crisis among our churches, and the 'Dega Mullet is a big part of the problem. Among the family of churches Derek and I belong to, the Southern Baptist Convention, discipleship has declined significantly over the past few decades. A 2018 report found that if SBC churches simply retained those they baptized, church attendance would double.[54]

Mullet Makeover: Christ-Centered Principles to Reshape Your Theology

If you are ready to get off the racetrack and leave the 'Dega Mullet behind, here are three Christ-centered principles that lead to finishing a more fulfilling race.

Wise, Not Witty

Everyone loves a good joke, but if you've ever been around a young child who tells the same joke over and over again, you know that wit can get old really fast. We've tried to teach our children this simple principle: "First time, funny. Second time, tolerated. Third time, annoying." Wit is great—unless you're looking for real substance and meaning. The cultural South is known for its wit. Love for the common man is woven into the fabric of the cultural South, and the common man is full of common sense and wit. Love for the common man and common sense are often accompanied by skepticism for higher education. We typically don't trust the fancy man in a fancy suit with a long title behind his name. In many cases, this has saved us a lot of

---

54 https://www.baptistpress.com/resource-library/news/task-force-report-baptism-must-lead-to-discipleship/.

heartache and pain. Education isn't everything. In fact, much of the educational system in our nation has been hijacked by elitists with very little wisdom. As we often say, they are educated beyond their intelligence.

But education and knowledge aren't the same thing. And the Bible elevates knowledge to a place of honor.

> The fear of the Lord is the beginning of knowledge; fools despise wisdom and instruction. **Proverbs 1:7**

> How long, O simple ones, will you love being simple? How long will scoffers delight in their scoffing and fools hate knowledge? **Proverbs 1:22**

> The beginning of wisdom is this: Get wisdom, and whatever you get, get insight. Prize her highly, and she will exalt you; she will honor you if you embrace her. She will place on your head a graceful garland; she will bestow on you a beautiful crown. **Proverbs 4:7–9**

We often think of Proverbs as a book about wisdom, and we think of wisdom as if it is somehow separate from knowledge. It's not. Yes, wisdom requires more than knowledge, but it certainly does not require less than knowledge. The more true knowledge we gain, the more we can apply that knowledge. Proverbs speaks as often about knowledge and insight as it does about wisdom.

The Bible describes Solomon's wisdom, and it includes knowledge about plants and animals that sounds like an ancient classification system.

> God gave Solomon wisdom and understanding beyond measure, and breadth of mind like the sand on the seashore . . . He spoke of trees, from the cedar that is in Lebanon to the hyssop that grows out of the wall. He spoke also of beasts, and of birds, and of reptiles, and of fish. **1 Kings 4:29, 33**

Wisdom is more than just common sense. In the cultural South, we exalt common sense but question anything that sounds too much like knowledge. This philosophy has greatly contributed to the 'Dega Mullet and its disdain for learning the things of God. We are to seek knowledge and grow in understanding. Paul tells us in Philippians that when we do what we have learned from those who follow Jesus, we will have peace from God. He says it this way:

> What you have learned and received and heard and seen in me—practice these things, and the God of peace will be with you. **Philippians 4:9**

In his letters to Titus and Timothy, Paul teaches that it is imperative to handle the Word of Truth rightly and to keep and teach sound doctrine so that it might lead to righteousness, completeness, and good works (2 Timothy 2:15, 3:16, and Titus 2:1). In Romans we learn that the instruction of Scripture is a source of hope for us, (Romans 15:4) and can keep us from conforming to the world (Romans 12:2). Paul instructed Timothy to build a culture of teaching and discipleship.

> What you have heard from me in the presence of many witnesses entrust to faithful men, who will be able to teach others also. **2 Timothy 2:2**

When we askew wisdom and knowledge in favor of common sense, we make ourselves vulnerable to the deception of the world around us. Common sense is often unbiblical thinking dressed in the garb of our culture.

If you still aren't convinced that you need to grow in wisdom, Luke's words should seal the deal.

> Jesus increased in wisdom and in stature and in favor with God and man. **Luke 2:52**

If Jesus needed to grow in wisdom, so do we.

Lord, Not Lapdog

To trim the unsightly 'Dega Mullet, we need to have a proper perspective. John Piper gave a practical parenting tip that I (Derek) have used with each of my children.[55] He suggested taking your child to a place with very tall buildings when your child is fairly young, around three to five years old. When you are still a good distance away from one of the tallest buildings, ask the child to show you how big the building is. They will likely use their hands, or even fingers if you are far enough away, to demonstrate the building's size. Then, take the child closer to the building—even close enough to touch it. Once again, ask the child to show you how big the building. As the child looks up, he will quickly realize his arms are no longer sufficient measuring sticks. Piper encouraged parents to use the teaching moment to remind

---

[55] "Ask Pastor John" podcast, episode unknown.

children (and ourselves) that the closer you are to something (or someone), the bigger they are. God is infinitely bigger than we could ever imagine, and if we think we can measure Him with our little minds, we are very far from Him.

Deep biblical truths cannot be diminished to cute sayings. The King of Kings, Lord of Lords, and the Creator God of the universe cannot be treated like one of our household pets. He's not cute. He's God. He's not a baby. He's God incarnate. We realize that no one reading this refers to Jesus in the way Ricky Bobby does, but "Dear Lord baby Jesus" is a caricature of southern culture. A caricature doesn't create features. It exaggerates them. In other words, if there wasn't some truth to the "Dear Lord baby Jesus" mindset, no one would find it funny. Compare "Dear Lord baby Jesus" to another description of Jesus as an infant.

> Christ, by highest heav'n adored
> Christ, the everlasting Lord!
> Late in time behold Him come
> Offspring of a virgin's womb
> Veiled in flesh the Godhead see
> Hail th' incarnate Deity
> Pleased as man with man to dwell
> Jesus our Immanuel.[56]

Baby Jesus in a manger does not seem threatening to anyone. That's why our culture prefers that picture of Jesus over the one of Jesus hanging on the cross or walking out of the tomb.

Jesus is the One whose thoughts are so much higher than ours that the distance has to be measured in atmospheres (Isaiah 55:9; Psalm 147:5). He is the God who created all things (Colossians 1:16), knows all things (Luke 12:7), and knows the why behind all things (Jeremiah 1:5). He is not a cute little baby, or even worse, a cute lap dog. If anyone is going to be in someone's lap, it would be us in His lap not Him in ours.

Follower, Not Fan

---

[56] Wesley, Charles, adapted by George Whitfield, "Hark The Herald Angels Sing," *Collection of Hymns for Social Worship*, 1754.
It is worth noting that Charles Wesley did not like Whitfield's changes. Charles had originally written "Hark how all the Welkin (heaven) rings" and was opposed to Hark the herald angels sing" because the Bible does not say the angels sang their message. Wesley's objections further exemplify the seriousness with which theology and biblical truth have been treated throughout Christian history.

In his book, *Not a Fan*, Kyle Idleman hits the nail on the head. He distinguishes between a follower of Jesus and a fan of Jesus. He writes:

> Fans don't mind him doing a little touch-up work, but Jesus wants complete renovation. Fans come to Jesus thinking tune-up, but Jesus is thinking overhaul. Fans think a little makeup is fine, but Jesus is thinking makeover. Fans think a little decorating is required, but Jesus wants a complete remodel. Fans want Jesus to inspire them, but Jesus wants to interfere with their lives.[57]

Jesus taught this over and over.

> Whoever loses his life for my sake will find it. **Matthew 10:39** (see also Matthew 16:25; Mark 8:35; Luke 9:24; John 12:25)

Yes, He is talking about physical death and eternal life, but Jesus is also teaching His followers that we are to lose our way of life for His sake and gain His way of life. This teaching of losing and finding life is preceded by Jesus urging the crowd to take up their cross, deny themselves, and follow Him (Mark 8:34). Then it is followed by Jesus's sobering question:

> For what does it profit a man to gain the whole world and forfeit his soul? **Mark 8:36**

In a similar book, *Follow Me: A Call to Die. A Call to Live.*, David Platt poignantly asks:

> Why are so many supposed Christians sitting on the sidelines of the church, maybe even involved in the machinery of the church, but not wholeheartedly, passionately, sacrificially, and joyfully giving their lives to making disciples of all the nations? Could it be because so many people in the church have settled for superficial religion instead of supernatural regeneration?[58]

---

[57] Kyle Idleman, *Not a Fan: Becoming a Completely Committed Follower of Jesus*, Updated, Expanded Edition (Grand Rapids, Michigan: Zondervan, 2016). 31.
[58] David Platt and Francis Chan, *Follow Me: A Call to Die. A Call to Live.*, Unabridged Edition (Carol Stream, IL: Tyndale Elevate, 2013), 69.

Jesus doesn't just want a relationship with you. He wants to regenerate you!

Release yourself from the binding contract you've had with these cheap sponsors. Wise up, die to yourself, and be raised to new life that can be found by following Jesus as Lord.

Chapter Eight: The Joe Dirt Mullet

Introduction

The 2001 film *Joe Dirt*, the title character is a hillbilly who had been abandoned by his parents when he was eight years old. The movie is full of crude and raunchy content as it follows his journey across the country to find his long-lost parents. His family life, along with every other part of his life, is a dirty mess. We have not seen this movie, and we don't recommend it. We do, however, think there's something to learn from it. According to movie critic, Steven Isaac:

> [Joe Dirt] leads moviegoers to a singular truth: Parents serve more than a biological function. They can make or break a young person's life by how they act, how they think and how they raise—or don't raise—their kids.[59]

Joe Dirt is more than just a guy with a classic mullet. He's an example of what happens when parents fail to fulfill their biblical roles.

Mullet Description

The Joe Dirt Mullet drops the kids off at church and might even come with them from time to time. Real family discipleship, however, is completely absent. The Joe Dirt Mullet keeps Jesus in the front by saying, "I will/am/did raise my kids in church" and keeps the party in the back by never taking on the responsibility of family discipleship. In many cases, the Joe Dirt Mullet lets the wife lead the

---

[59] https://www.pluggedin.com/movie-reviews/joedirt/.

way spiritually while the husband spends his time pursuing work or hobbies. The Joe Dirt Mullet is known for a shorter front and a longer back. We feel that is fitting for this grimy theology. There's just enough Jesus in the front to check the "church" box while leaving plenty of time and energy for the party in the back. Parents who wear the Joe Dirt Mullet are often caught off guard when their children descend into all manner of immorality, brokenness, confusion, and sin. They feel like they did a decent job raising them the right way, and they don't see the connection between the lack of family discipleship and the shattered family.

Before describing some of the places we've seen the Joe Dirt Mullet in its natural habitat, let me be clear. Raising your children in a godly, biblical home with intentional and consistent discipleship does not guarantee they will always follow Jesus. Some people misapply Proverbs 22:6, "Train up a child in the way he should go; even when he is old he will not depart from it." They read it as a promise that children raised in church will always be followers of Christ.

First, this is not a promise. It's a proverb. A proverb is a statement of wisdom which is generally true. It is not a rule or a law or a formula. It is generally true that children raised in a God-honoring home will grow up to honor God. Second, the proverb refers to "when he is old," and sometimes, children raised in good homes drift away from the faith only to come back later in life. That doesn't mean there won't be significant periods of brokenness and rebellion between the "train up" and "not depart." Finally, some have translated this proverb to say, "Train up a child in the way he is bent." In other words, it's possible this proverb has more to do with understanding the unique strengths, weaknesses, and personality of each child and parenting him in a way that works best with those characteristics.

There are no perfect parents, and great parents don't always produce godly children. Each person must make his or her own choices. Christian history is filled with examples of those who grew up in solid Christian homes only to walk away from the faith. It is also filled with stories of men and women who were not raised in Christian homes but lived as sold-out followers of Jesus. There are no perfect parents, but there is a perfect Father. He created two people, provided everything they needed, put them in a perfect place, and spent time with them—they still rebelled.

Avoiding the Joe Dirt Mullet is not about the product—godly children. It's about the process—serious spiritual leadership and discipleship of children. Those who have invested in and discipled their children in a way that honors the Lord cannot feel guilty if those children choose a different path in life. Conversely, parents who ignore or casually approach the discipleship of their children are sporting the Joe Dirt Mullet even if their children turn out to be solid followers of Jesus.

Mullet Sightings

"All's I got to do is keep bein' a good person. No matter what, good things'll come my way. Everything's gonna happen for me, just so long as I never have 'No' in my heart." Joe Dirt.[60]

The Joe Dirt Mullet shares a strong family resemblance to its cousin, the 'Dega Mullet. What distinguishes the Joe Dirt Mullet from others, however, is the passive role of parents, and specifically fathers, in leading and discipling their families. Consider some of the Joe Dirt Mullet's favorite sayings.

"My church is in a deer stand" or **"I'm closer to God in the woods than anywhere else."** These statements have been made by countless southern men when questioned about their lack of involvement in a local church. They try to defend their absenteeism and keep a little Jesus in the front by claiming to worship the Lord better out in "His creation." They tell their families weekend after weekend, **"I'll be at the deer camp if you need me."** And they do need him, but they don't have him because he's at the deer camp. They need him on a steady and consistent basis, but he isn't there protecting, pastoring, or leading his family. He is leaving them vulnerable for any of the countless attacks the enemy could send their way, and he has no idea.

Now, the Joe Dirt Mullet keeps the Jesus in front by being proud of his wife and kids for attending church. He believes that's just where they should be. He often says it this way, **"Church is for women and kids; my church is right here in my recliner."** As long as the wife doesn't give too much of his money to the church and his kids can still be the star athletes on travel ball teams, the Joe Dirt Mullet has no issue with his family attending the church down the street. He might even come with them on special occasions as long as there's not an important game happening at the same time.

The Joe Dirt Mullet has a backwards view on raising children. It views children as a lifestyle killer and a large family as a burden rather than a blessing. Derek and I have five children. We've lost count of the number of times we've heard, **"You need a new hobby, don't you**

---

[60] *Joe Dirt*, Columbia Pictures, 2001.

know what causes that?" Actually, we do know what causes it, and we enjoy our "hobby." We don't need or want a new one.

Unfortunately, we've often heard this from within the church. It seems harmless and fun, but it subtly communicates "Big families are weird. Kids are a burden. Stinks for you." Anna, a sweet friend of mine and mother of eight, expressed her fatigue from continually hearing similar comments. She said, "You can see a stark difference in the amount of sincere congratulations and applause you receive when you announce a certain accumulation of wealth or successful achievement in comparison to that of a new child. It's a huge difference!"

There comes a day in the life of every Joe Dirt Mullet when they look out from the deer stand or away from the TV and notice their family is gone. Sometimes figuratively, some times literally. They find their children have become adults with zero moral compass. They are battling addictions, suicidal behaviors, endless debt, and toxic relationships. They just scratch their mullets and say, **"I don't know why they are living like that. They were raised in church!"**

Mullet Dangers

The dangers of the Joe Dirt Mullet almost seem so obvious they don't need to be mentioned, but if that were the case we wouldn't need to write the book, right? This mullet is extremely dangerous because it directly affects not only the wearer, but also those closest to him. This is a battle for the family. The Joe Dirt Mullet destroys families. Plain and simple.

Focus on the Family is an organization that has been striving to serve Christian families since 1977 with resources that can help strengthen marriages, families, churches, and communities. Within their values they declare,

> Ultimately, we believe the purpose of life is to know and glorify God through an authentic relationship with His Son, Jesus Christ. This purpose is lived out first within our own families then extended, in love, to an increasingly broken world that desperately needs Him.[61]

The enemy knows very well that a broken family leads to a broken world. Over and over, we see the family is most easily broken when its leadership is broken. Parents, and more specifically fathers,

---

[61] "Foundational Values," Focus on the Family, accessed February 8, 2023, https://www.focusonthefamily.com/about/foundational-values/.

who choose selfishness over serving, laziness over leading, and passivity over passion will find themselves smack dab in the middle of the path of destruction. And they will drag their kids right along with them. Before they know it, the family will be so far removed from abundant life and joy that they can't even see how to get back to it.

Mullet Makeover: Christ-Centered Principles to Reshape Your Theology

The church is not a building. That's true. But the church is not found in isolation or out somewhere in nature alone. The church, when spoken of in Scripture, is always speaking of the gathered and collaborative people of God. The Bible continually speaks of God's people as sheep and the Lord as our Shepherd. Just as sheep thrive in a herd under the protection and guidance of their shepherd, we were created to live in community with one another under the leadership of our Lord Jesus Christ on the path to life that He laid out for us. What are some principles on that path of life that can better shape our theology?

Church is Not a Place

When the Joe Dirt Mullet thinks about church, it thinks about a place. If church is just a building, then it can be a deer stand or a recliner. It's no wonder the Joe Dirt Mullet fails to see the value and power of the real church. Buildings crumble, deer stands rust, and recliners usually end up with rips repaired by duct tape. Where's the power in that? There isn't any! But the real church is defined by Scripture as the body of Christ. Romans 12 speaks to this beginning in verse four saying,

> For as in one body we have many members, and the members do not all have the same function, so we, though many, are one body in Christ, and individually members one of another. Having gifts that differ according to the grace given to us, let us use them: if prophecy, in proportion to our faith; if service, in our serving; the one who teaches, in his teaching; the one who exhorts, in his exhortation; the one who contributes, in generosity; the one who leads, with zeal; the one who does acts of mercy, with cheerfulness. **Romans 12:4–8**

First Corinthians 12 echoes the same idea and adds,

> For the body does not consist of one member but of many. If the foot should say, "Because I am not a hand, I do not belong to the body," that would not make it any less a part of the body. And if the ear should say, "Because I am not an eye, I do not belong to the body," that would not make it any less a part of the body. If the whole body were an eye, where would be the sense of hearing? If the whole body were an ear, where would be the sense of smell? But as it is, God arranged the members in the body, each one of them, as he chose. If all were a single member, where would the body be? As it is, there are many parts, yet one body. The eye cannot say to the hand, "I have no need of you," nor again the head to the feet, "I have no need of you." On the contrary, the parts of the body that seem to be weaker are indispensable, and on those parts of the body that we think less honorable we bestow the greater honor, and our unpresentable parts are treated with greater modesty, which our more presentable parts do not require. But God has so composed the body, giving greater honor to the part that lacked it, that there may be no division in the body, but that the members may have the same care for one another. If one member suffers, all suffer together; if one member is honored, all rejoice together. **1 Corinthians 12:14–26**

In both passages, Paul teaches that we cannot just decide we don't matter to the church or the church doesn't matter to us. God designed His people to serve one another in unity. You can't serve others and live in unity alone! It is a selfish person who says, "I don't need the church." That might sound like a statement of strength, but it's just the opposite. It's like a toddler who is gaining independence and wants to do everything themselves. It might be a little cute at first, but there comes a point when the loving parents must draw some clear lines. Trust me. Letting a two-year-old wipe themselves after using the potty without a parent making sure it was done properly negatively affects everyone around.

Shifting your theology from "going to church" to "being part of the church" can make all the difference! Open your eyes to see the value of being a part of the body of Christ. Engage in a local church through worship, small groups, serving, and missions. You have gifts to offer to a local body of believers that will help them grow, and they have gifts to offer that will help you and your family grow. It's a win-win!

That's one of the reasons the author of Hebrews commands us to gather with other believers regularly.

> Let us consider how to stir up one another to love and good works, not neglecting to meet together, as is the habit of some, but encouraging one another. **Hebrews 10:24–25**

Walk in Integrity

One of my (Lindsay's) high school teachers used to tell us that integrity is doing the right thing even when you think no one is looking. That definition has come to my mind often. It has even helped me do the right thing even when I didn't think anyone was looking. The word "think" is very key in this definition. The Joe Dirt Mullet lives with the delusion that his mullet is his business and it only affects him.

If you've lived long enough, you have probably had an embarrassing fall at some point. One of the first thoughts that goes through your mind after a fall is, "Did anybody see that?" Most of the time, the answer is, unfortunately, yes. We cannot live our lives believing that no one else is watching. We also can't believe the lie that our actions (or lack of actions) only matter to us. Especially as parents, we have a constant audience. The decisions we make today absolutely affect and shape the tomorrow of our children, but our actions also shape their today.

Sometimes parents think, "When they get a little older, I will really buckle down and take this whole Jesus thing a little more seriously." Unfortunately, habits are formed and patterns are set that have pointed the family on a trajectory of death rather than life. Proverbs teaches a beautiful principle regarding integrity.

> The righteous who walks in his integrity—blessed are his children after him! **Proverbs 20:7**

Do you see how a father's integrity blesses future generations?

"Fathering Strong: The Real Epidemic of Today" analyzes results from the 2020 census data on fatherhood to paint a sobering picture of the current crisis.[62] Among other statistics, the census found that the absence of a father directly correlates to higher rates of depression, suicide, substance abuse, crime, early sexual activity, and poor educational outcomes among children. In contrast, children growing up in homes with fathers present experience a better ability to

---

[62] fatheringstrong.com, https://heyzine.com/flip-book/2b7a98ad3f.html#page/1.

control their emotions, better physical health, healthier relationships, less use of drugs and alcohol, better school performance, and more sense of safety and confidence.

Children need their parents, and especially their fathers, to be present in their lives, walking in integrity. They are watching! They see much more than you realize, and it deeply affects them now and will continue to shape them in the future. If church is an afterthought for you, it will likely be an afterthought for them. If Jesus is not Lord of your life, He is less likely to be Lord of their lives. If you do not take the path of life seriously, they are more likely to follow you down the path of destruction. Men, you are the spiritual leaders of your families. Where are you leading them to?

Do Not Provoke

In his letters to the church at Ephesus and Colossae, the Apostle Paul wrote,

> Fathers, do not provoke your children to anger, but bring them up in the discipline and instruction of the Lord. **Ephesians 6:4**

> Fathers, do not provoke your children, lest they become discouraged. **Colossians 3:21**

The Greek word for *father* used in these verses can also be translated as *parents*.[63] In their incredibly practical and helpful book, *The Faithful Parent*, Martha Peace and Stuart Scott identify fifteen types of parents that provoke children to anger.[64] They write,

> Although there are times that a young person is sinfully angry without being provoked by a parent, there are many parents who do provoke their children. Both parent and child must assume responsibility for their actions, but a provoking parent holds the greater responsibility in the breakdown of unity.[65]

Peace and Scott's fifteen types of provoking parents are:

- The proud parent
- The despairing parent
- The controlling/angry parent

---

[63] James Strong, *The New Strong's Dictionary of the Words in the Greek Testament* (Nashville, TN: Thomas Nelson, 1995), 69 (#3962).
[64] Martha Peace and Stuart Scott, *The Faithful Parent: A Biblical Guide to Raising a Family* (Phillipsburg, N.J: P & R Publishing, 2010), 127-142.
[65] Peace and Scott, *The Faithful Parent*, 142.

- The "guess what the rules are today?" parent
- The exaggerating parent
- The "must be perfect" parent
- The "fear of what my child and others might think" parent
- The submissive/easily manipulated parent
- The "why can't you be like your brother?" parent
- The "let me live the life I've always wanted through you" parent
- The "hands-off and let the child decide" parent
- The tradition—or culture—driven parent
- The omniscient/presumptuous parent
- The "if love is there, it is a secret" parent
- The "preoccupied by so many things" parent

Although I highly recommend reading the book, you don't have to read the full descriptions before seeing yourself in one or more of them. I know I did!

Consider Yourself a Trainer

Remember Proverbs 22:6, "Train up a child in the way he should go; even when he is old he will not depart from it"? Many people quote this verse when holding on to hope that their prodigal will come to his or her senses. As mentioned above, many prodigals have rejected the diligent training and warnings of their godly parents. This is not speaking to those circumstances.

In the case of cultural Christianity, the Joe Dirt Mullet lies to parents about this verse. It makes them think that passively allowing their children to participate in church functions from time to time, or even forcing steady church attendance, is equivalent to training up a child in the way he should go. Church attendance is part of training up a child in the way he should go, but it is only a part.

The Joe Dirt Mullet style of parenting is like a personal trainer who drops his clients off at the gym and waits in the parking lot. Hopefully, the gym has machines with clear instructions. If the client is very dedicated, he or she might see a few results and meet a few goals. The personal trainer, however, cannot share in the joy of those achieved goals, and frankly, shouldn't be paid for them either. If the client doesn't achieve his or her goals and asks for a refund, the trainer has no right to say, "But I took you to the gym." Our kids need disciplers, not Uber drivers.

The church is not called, designed, or equipped to function as a parent. God has trusted the discipleship of our children to us, the parents, and has blessed us with the church to offer support in that role. Of course, many strong believers over the years have attributed their spiritual growth to a faithful church member who discipled them. Thank God for that! But the math just doesn't work.

While pastors and church leaders often invest in a few children and students on a deeper level, there aren't enough hours in the day to disciple each child and student adequately. It is also not their job. What happens when the family has to move due to a job change? What about the late hours of the night when the child is struggling with life's biggest questions? Who is there to disciple the child? It takes dedication and work on the parents' part to train their child. It means late nights, long and frequent conversations, modeling humility, faith, and spiritual disciplines in front of the child, and seeking the guidance of the Holy Spirit to disciple children. It also requires help. Many times that help comes from the encouragement of fellow believers walking through the similar seasons of life. This is another reason why the church is just as vital for parents as it is for kids.

Why do you believe the Bible is true? John Piper, who we've referenced often in this book, was once asked that question. John has a brilliant mind and significant theological training. His answer will probably surprise you. He responded, "Why does John Piper believe the Bible is true? Because my mother told me so." Grateful for his mother's influence, Pastor John gave a message in 2012 at the Bethlehem Women's Conference on the indispensable priority of the Bible. In that message, John said, "Nothing is more crucial for being the woman God made you to be and knowing how to make your life count than being saturated with the Bible."[66] When parents lead the way in discipling their children, they also lead the way in sharing the joy of the fruit of that child's faith. I cannot imagine how proud John Piper's mother was as she witnessed her son's life and ministry. John the Apostle said it this way:

> I have no greater joy than to hear that my children are walking in the truth. **3 John 1:4**

Joe Dirt didn't get everything wrong. In the movie, Joe says, "Life is too short to waste doing nothing, make everyday count because we all don't know when we will leave this world." The way to make life count is not the YOLO (you only live once) mentality that pursues dreams, a career, or a hobby. The way to make life count is pursuing

---

[66] Jonathan Parnell, "My Mama Told Me It Was So," *Desiring God* (blog), May 13, 2012, https://www.desiringgod.org/articles/my-mama-told-me-it-was-so.

the gospel and bringing your family along with you. Jesus said it this way:

> Do not lay up for yourselves treasures on earth, where moth and rust destroy and where thieves break in and steal, but lay up for yourselves treasures in heaven, where neither moth nor rust destroys and where thieves do not break in and steal. For where your treasure is, there your heart will be also.
> **Matthew 6:19–21**

Chapter Nine: It's Time For a Haircut

Have you ever seen a crazy mullet and wondered, "How can they think *that* looks good?" Us too. Here's the thing—style is determined by influence. The people around us and the media we consume develop our sense of style. What you and I might think is an atrocious, over the top, crazy mullet might be all the rage at the local high school.

Three Theological Styles

The same is true of theology. The people we surround ourselves with and the ideas we entertain eventually shape the way we think about God, Jesus, and the Christian life. They create our theological style, and that can lead to theological mullets. There are three styles that can produce a Jesus in the front, party in the back wreck of a theological hairdo. We've labeled them the Cool Style, The Baby Style, and the Comeback Style. Any of the eight mullets catalogued in the previous chapters can result from embracing one of the three styles.

The Cool Style

The Cool Style is just that—cool. At least it's cool to you and your friends. We embrace this style when we are so immersed in the culture around us that we think it's just the way things are supposed to be. All the cool kids do it.

Those who are driven by the Cool Style have bought into the image the culture sells them—they are simply going with the mullet flow. They have been discipled by music, movies, media, and the cultural norms around them rather than Jesus and His followers. The more a person has been surrounded by cultural Christianity, the more he will think a theological mullet is cool. The Cool Style will make a cultural Christian feel right at home among all the other mullet wearers. For many people, comfort is found in numbers, so when mullets are all they see, they just join right in without a thought.

The Baby Style

We have all seen a baby mullet, and we must admit, they are the cutest of all mullets. Baby mullets are unlike any other mullet because they grow naturally, and they can sneak up on us. If Mom and Dad wait too long to get the baby's first haircut, the baby mullet will make an appearance. Their little hair grows in funny ways the first year or so of their life, and it can be so hard to part with those precious little locks!

The Baby Style produces theological mullets because we are not paying attention. It grows in our theological blind spots. The good news is that it only takes a few cuts to get that baby looking spiffy again! You just have to be willing to part with the sacred curls that have formed at the bottom.

The Comeback Style

Just when we all thought the mullet was the thing of the past, suddenly it resurfaced with the next generation. How could it be that in 2023 we are seeing more mullets than ever? It is because whether they admit it or not, younger generations are greatly influenced by the generations before them. In terms of theology, the Comeback Style exists because the issues of the older generations have not been properly addressed. Like a bad hairstyle, these issues keep coming back. They seem to cycle through each generation, and they can occur in even stranger and bolder forms.

The Comeback Style can be a result of how we were raised, and you can't control the theological environment you were raised in. Perhaps you've grown a theological mullet because your parents weren't intentional about discipling you. Or maybe the influence of your parents was drowned out by the influence of your friends and community. In some cases, the church you were raised in might have contributed to a theological mullet. We have very little control over our theological influences when we are children. If you're old enough to read this book, however, you're old enough to change that.

If it was bad theology for the last generation, it's bad theology for you. It does not need to come back. We can let it die. But if we fail to intentionally groom our thoughts, influences, and habits we will find ourselves thinking and believing things that are not biblically sound. Bad theology has a way of showing up over and over again.

CUT IT

You might find yourself at the end of this book wondering where to go from here. Let us encourage you—you don't have to go on saying or believing wrong things! Don't be like Pilate when he asked the question, "What is truth?" The embodiment of Truth was standing right in front of him (John 18:37–38)! He ignored the revealed Word of God. He acted out of his own desire and for his own selfish benefit. Rather, be the kind of person who, when faced with Truth, recognizes it and acts upon it. Take a look in the spiritual mirror right now. Go ahead. Look closely. Use multiple mirrors if necessary so you can see all the angles. Do you see a mullet? CUT IT!

Count the costs.
Understand your influences.
Think about eternal things.

Investigate the Scriptures.
Train yourself in godliness.

Count the Costs

Change is hard. Cutting away sloppy theology can often result in tension in relationships, loss of friendships, awkwardness in social situations, and ultimately death to your selfishness. It can get expensive. Our brothers and sisters in the persecuted church understand the great cost of accepting salvation and choosing a life of following Christ. For many of them, becoming a follower of Jesus means they will lose their family, jobs, citizenship, honor, or even their lives. Jesus taught it this way:

> If anyone comes to me and does not hate his own father and mother and wife and children and brothers and sisters, yes, and even his own life, he cannot be my disciple. Whoever does not bear his own cross and come after me cannot be my disciple. For which of you, desiring to build a tower, does not first sit down and count the cost, whether he has enough to complete it? Otherwise, when he has laid a foundation and is not able to finish, all who see it begin to mock him, saying, "This man began to build and was not able to finish." Or what king, going out to encounter another king in war, will not sit down first and deliberate whether he is able with ten thousand to meet

him who comes against him with twenty thousand? And if not, while the other is yet a great way off, he sends a delegation and asks for terms of peace. So therefore, any one of you who does not renounce all that he has cannot be my disciple.
Luke 14:26–33

In the American church, we like to say, "Jesus doesn't ask everyone to give up family, jobs, wealth, comfort, etc., but if He does, we should be ready." Allow us to push back on that thinking a tad. That's the safe thinking that has led to much of the mullet mania in cultural Christianity.

Many Christians assume that serious sacrifice is only for a handful of super Christians. That's a dull and cheapened view of salvation. As Francis Chan says:

> I quickly found that the American church is a difficult place to fit in if you want to live out New Testament Christianity. The goals of American Christianity are often a nice marriage, children who don't swear, and good church attendance. Taking the words of Christ literally, and seriously, is rarely considered. That's for the 'radicals' who are 'unbalanced' and who go 'overboard.' Most of us want a balanced life we can control, that is safe, and that does not involve suffering.[67]

In contrast, when we look at the early church, we see a group of people who gave everything for the sake of the gospel and its advancement. Ten of the twelve original followers of Jesus willingly accepted martyrdom. Countless others throughout the generations have given their lives to advance the gospel, build the church, and preserve Scripture.

The call to follow Jesus is the call to lay the blank check of our life on the table for God to fill in. We willingly submit ourselves to Him knowing He might ask us to do something we would not choose for ourselves. We trust that He has information we don't, and whatever He asks of us is for our eternal good and His eternal glory. That's the promise. It is not our safety or our prosperity or that we will be spared from suffering. Instead, God promises us that whatever He allows us to experience and endure is used to shape us into the image of Jesus.

---

[67] Francis Chan, Chris Tomlin, and Danae Yankoski, *Crazy Love: Overwhelmed by a Relentless God*, New, Revised and Updated Edition (Colorado Springs, CO: David C Cook, 2013), 68.

And we know that for those who love God all things work together for good, for those who are called according to his purpose. For those whom he foreknew he also predestined to be conformed to the image of his Son. **Romans 8:28–29**

A new airline came to our town recently. It's similar to another well-known airline which boasts of cheap fares. A ticket on this airline seems like an amazing deal because of the initial price. Eventually, the price evens out as passengers are charged additional fees for every single thing imaginable. No kidding, this new airline charges a base fee to get on the plane, but then you are required to pay an additional fee to have a seat. Not to pick your seat . . . just to *have* a seat. As my husband says, "That's how they getcha." I think cultural Christianity has laid a similar spiritual trap for many people. They are told they can just repeat some words and go to Heaven one day. No life change required. Many Christians are surprised to learn that Jesus actually requires much more from us. In fact, He requires all we have and all we are.

We need more voices of truth helping us consider the actual cost of following Jesus. In *Counter Culture*, David Platt writes

> In a world where everything revolves around yourself—protect yourself, promote yourself, comfort yourself, and take care of yourself—Jesus says, "Crucify yourself." Put aside all self-preservation in order to live for God's glorification, no matter what that means for you in the culture around you.[68]

Francis Chan echoes that thought. "The world says love yourself, grab all you can, follow your heart. Jesus says deny yourself, grab your cross, and follow me."[69] We don't want to use the "gotcha" technique when bringing people to Christ. That is how we end up with so many mullets. Instead, we need true followers of Christ to help the lost and dying world consider the full cost of following Jesus while also considering the overwhelming reward.

Understand Your Influence

Influence works two ways in your life. You are influenced, and you are an influencer. When it comes to Mullet Theology, both matter.

---

[68] David Platt, *Counter Culture: Following Christ in an Anti-Christian Age*, Revised Edition (Carol Stream, IL: Tyndale Elevate, 2017), xiv.
[69] Chan, Tomlin, and Yankoski, *Crazy Love*. https://www.azquotes.com/quote/1411292

Who influences you? The voices you allow into your life make a difference in who you are and how you live. Chances are, you don't wear the same clothes you wore, and you don't have the same hairstyle you had in high school. Why not? Weren't they cool? Oh, that style was really cool according to a small group of people (your friends) in a small geographical region (your high school). When you see a teenager with an appalling mullet, don't forget, he thinks it's cool because his friends think it's cool.

If you don't understand why you think and live the way you think and live, you will never change the way you think and live. Outside of the Holy Spirit's work inside of us, the voices we allow into our lives have more power over us than anything else. If you want to get in shape, start hanging out with people who are in shape. Read what they read. Listen to what they listen to. Watch what they watch. Eventually, you will find yourself doing what they do. The same is true for theology and the Christian life.

What did you watch, listen to, and read today? Who did you spend time with this week? Are the influences you're allowing into your life pointing you toward a deeper walk with the Lord? If you acted like the people in the songs, movies, and social media posts you consumed this week, would you be more like Jesus or less like Jesus? If you became more like your closest friends, would you be a more godly man or woman?

The influences you allow into your life are important. It is also important to see yourself as an influencer. Most people don't think of themselves as influencers, but the truth is, everyone influences someone! The definition of an influencer is "One who inspires or guides the actions of others."[70] We all play a part in the decisions others make. If you are a parent, you have massive influence over your children. Like it or not, your children form their worldviews based largely on your influence. All of the things they first consider right and good and normal are formed by observing you.

Parents are not the only influencers. If you have a friend, you are an influencer. If you go out in public, travel on public transportation, attend a sporting event, or even go to a gas station, you are an influencer. Most people want to sink into the crowd and follow the influence of the culture and hope to not be noticed. This is still influencing! You can't escape it. If you are thinking like everyone else, speaking like everyone else, dressing like everyone else, and behaving

---

[70] https://www.merriam-webster.com/dictionary/influencer

like everyone else, you are a part of the larger voice that is echoing the influence of the culture, "This is what's good, accepted, and desirable."

You can't choose not to be an influencer, but you can choose to be intentional about your influence. What if you took seriously the commands of Jesus and allowed those commands to shape your thoughts, speech, dress, and behavior? It would not go unnoticed! People would notice the change and have one of three reactions. Some people would be offended by it and feel judged or guilty for their behaviors; they would criticize and even ostracize and persecute you. Other people would be convicted by it and feel empowered to follow your lead. Still others would be encouraged because they would no longer feel alone in their convictions.

If you live for Christ, you will face criticism. First Corinthians 1:18 warns us that the gospel will be offensive to those who do not understand it. This is such good news for us! We should be strengthened in our faith when the very thing Jesus told us would happen comes to fruition. Because Jesus also told us not to be afraid of this, we should have a renewed sense of courage when it happens.

In the world you will have tribulation. But take heart; I have overcome the world. **John 16:33**

When others persecute us for living for Jesus, we can praise God! When others are convicted and follow us, we can praise God! When believers are encouraged, we can praise God! Using your influence for Jesus is always a win-win.

Think About Eternal Things

In his dramatic satire, *The Screwtape Letters*, C. S. Lewis depicts Satan's master plan for keeping humans far from God and filling hell. He uses a series of letters from a seasoned demon to a new demon recruit. He writes, "It is funny how mortals always picture us as putting things into their minds: in reality our best work is done by keeping things out."[71] Isn't it true? Many people spend time filling their minds with things that have no real significance. We fill our heads with the "wood, hay, and straw" instead of "gold, silver, and precious stones" of 1 Corinthians 3.[72] It is a powerful thing to interject meaningful content into a conversation. Most conversations are naturally surface level and empty, so it takes effort to invite someone to think about ideas like

---

[71] C. S. Lewis, *The Screwtape Letters*, C. S. Lewis Signature Classic (London, England: William Collins, 2012), 16.
[72] 1 Corinthians 3:12–15

origins, truth, love, marriage, moral right and wrong, the dignity of human life, faithfulness, justice, virtue, ethics, liberty, and so many more. We will certainly not invite others to discuss these ideas if we are not thinking of them.

This goes back to our influences. We talk about what we think about. We think about what we fill our eyes and ears with. In an on-demand entertainment world, our eyes and ears are filled with memes, Fail Army videos, puppet-like politicians, home decorating ideas, graphic scenes, explicit lyrics, and even pictures of everyone's dinner for the night. Our world is full of filters and deep fakes, which causes our understanding of reality to be dangerously distorted. In 1986, Neil Postman sounded a sobering alarm about the influence of the entertainment world. In *Amusing Ourselves to Death*, he wrote,

> There is nothing wrong with entertainment. As some psychiatrist once put it, we all build castles in the air. The problems come when we try to live in them.[73]

Postman wrote those words in 1986 before the internet. Before social media. Before smartphones. Before on-demand streaming services. He was a voice crying out in the wilderness of the 1980s' entertainment world, and he was a prophet of things to come. Castles in the air—that's what the twenty-first century feels like. It seems everyone is building lives in the clouds and they are filling their days with nothing but mist and vapors.

Instead, brothers and sisters in Christ, we have such rich truths to soak in! We have an incredible inheritance to meditate upon, and we have such meaningful work to be doing. Think about the words of Paul to the church at Ephesus.

> Look carefully then how you walk, not as unwise but as wise, making the best use of the time, because the days are evil. Therefore do not be foolish, but understand what the will of the Lord is. **Ephesians 5:15–17**

We need to take our thoughts captive (2 Corinthians 10:4–5) and train our brains to be actively thinking on things that are worth thinking about.

---

[73] Neil Postman,. *Amusing Ourselves to Death* (New York, NY: Penguin, 1986), 77.

What are those things?

> Finally, brothers, whatever is true, whatever is honorable, whatever is just, whatever is pure, whatever is lovely, whatever is commendable, if there is any excellence, if there is anything worthy of praise, think about these things. **Philippians 4:8**

It could be helpful to keep a thought log for a few days to evaluate the things you spend your time thinking about. Get a notebook with some blank paper inside. At the beginning and end of each day, take about three minutes to do a brain-emptying session. Set a timer, and for three minutes in the morning, write all the things swimming around in your mind. It can be messy and all over the page. Don't think list. Think the word cloud. It might be things you need to get done, something you dreamed about the night before, a song running through your mind, a show or video you've watched that is sticking with you, or a meme you are still laughing at. Anything that pops into your mind is free game to jot down. You can pick a word or two to represent the thought. Don't feel the need to write sentences or paragraphs. Then, do the same thing in the evening before bed. This time, use your three minutes to remember as best you can the things you spent time thinking about during the day. Work problems and solutions, recipes, text conversations, articles or news stories, bills due or appointments coming up might be some examples of thought holders. Make a goal to see your output become less self-centered and shallow and more God-centered and glorious.

How can you control your thoughts? Change your input! Spend more time reading, listening to, and watching things that edify Christ and encourage you to live in a way that obeys His commands. This will mean removing other things to make space. Checking your phone's screen time can be a sober wake up call. The data doesn't lie. How many hours a day do you spend looking at things that feed your flesh rather than your spirit?

Investigate the Scriptures

In the early church, there was a special group of people called the Bereans.

> The brothers immediately sent Paul and Silas away by night to Berea, and when they arrived they went into the Jewish synagogue. Now these Jews were more noble than those in Thessalonica; they received the word with all eagerness, examining the Scriptures daily to see if these things were so.

> Many of them therefore believed, with not a few Greek women of high standing as well as men. **Acts 17:10–12**

This group had some specific qualities worth noting. First, they received the Word with all eagerness. This is the difference in having a hunger for God's Word versus just swallowing what's spoon fed to you. When we have an eagerness to know Scripture for ourselves, rapid spiritual growth is sure to follow. Second, they examined the Scriptures daily to see if things were so. This shows that Scripture was their standard of truth and it required daily examination to determine right from wrong, good from evil, truth from lie. Because of their daily pursuit of God's Word, they had no trouble believing. Even the most noble among them, the leaders and high ranking "bigwigs" if you will, had strong faith because they were rooted in a deep interaction with and understanding of Scripture. If believers followed the example of the Bereans, the mullets would just slide right off. They wouldn't have a chance to grow in the first place.

Train Yourself in Godliness

There comes a point when you move past thinking and start doing. Thinking is important, but if it never moves you to action, does it matter?

> But be doers of the word, and not hearers only, deceiving yourselves. **James 1:22**

When you begin the training process, there are a few things that will ensure better results. Just as in athletic training, spiritual training is more successful when you have accountability (a church family), access to equipment (Bible and study tools), realistic goals (small steps of growth), a plan (spiritual disciplines), and patience when it's not easy.

Remember this is a marathon, not a sprint. I once heard a pastor describe the Christian journey like this: some days we are running toward the finish line of faith, other days we are walking, still other days we are crawling, and on the extremely difficult days we are standing still; but we are always facing the goal. We are determined to move toward our beloved Savior, Jesus Christ, and He will bring us all the way to "Well done." As it is written,

> And let us not grow weary of doing good, for in due season we will reap, if we do not give up. **Galatians 6:9**

Conclusion

We love the fine folks of the South. Both of us can say, "I am one of you." That is one of the big reasons we wrote this book. We have a strong desire to see the people of the South awakened to the gospel once again. The cultural South is filled with more Kingdom resources than any other geographical region in history. If the hearts and resources of the cultural South are mobilized for the gospel, we can be an even larger part of successfully spreading the hope of salvation to people all over the world.

The world doesn't need watered-down sweet tea; nobody needs that. Neither does the world does need a mullet version of the gospel. We pray that the Lord might use this book to awaken your soul, and, in effect, awaken the soul of the cultural South. Our hope is that this awakening would press back even just a sliver of the darkness that has crept into our homes, neighborhoods, and even churches. Southern friends, lose the mullets, abandon the toxic parts of our culture, and wholeheartedly pursue the Great Commission.

> Now the eleven disciples went to Galilee, to the mountain to which Jesus had directed them. And when they saw him they worshiped him, but some doubted. And Jesus came and said to them, "All authority in heaven and on earth has been given to me. Go therefore and make disciples of all nations, baptizing them in the name of the Father and of the Son and of the Holy Spirit, teaching them to observe all that I have commanded you. And behold, I am with you always, to the end of the age.
> **Matthew 28:16–20**

Appendix: A Look in the Mirror

To help you identify any mullets that might be hanging around in your theology, we put together this questionnaire. It can help you quickly identify mullets you might be wearing. In the blank beside each statement, write a 1-5 using the following scale:

1 - Never
2 - Almost Never
3 - Sometimes
4 - Often
5 - Always

Answer quickly and honestly to find out if you have some party in the back that needs to be addressed. Total the answers from each section to find out if one or more of the mullets matches your theological style.

1–5, Looking Good
6–10, The Back Might Need a Little Trim
11–15, You're Rocking a Mullet
16–20, You're in the Mullet Hall of Fame

There's a separate questionnaire for each mullet discussed in the book, and the entire survey should only take about fifteen or twenty minutes.

Monster Ballad Mullet

___ I give advice about love, romance, and marriage that is more aligned with the culture than with Christ.

___ I believe love will guide the way through emotional connection and physical chemistry.

___ I believe the key to life is doing what makes you happy.

___ I believe if your spouse does not make you happy, your spouse is no longer right for you.

___ If you're in a loveless marriage, I think you should leave.

___ **Total**

'Merica Mullet

___ "God Bless the USA" moves me emotionally, but I'm not often moved by songs about Jesus.

___ I believe America has a special place in God's plan similar to the way He has a special plan for Israel.

___ The political party I support has no serious sin issues that need to be confronted.

___ I expect a special "patriotic service" at my church near the 4th of July, Veteran's Day, and/or Memorial Day that focuses on America and its servicemen and women.

___ I expect the American flag to be in a prominent position on the worship stage at my church.

___ **Total**

Wrastlin' Mullet

___ I just tell it like it is.

___ I think people need to just understand I am a blunt person, and they need to get over it if they don't like it.

___ I ain't gonna change for nobody.

___ I sit in the same seat in Sunday school and in the worship service each week, and I would not be happy if a guest was sitting there instead this Sunday.

___ I expect a convenient parking spot, hot coffee, and good seat at church.

___ Total

The Billy Ray Mullet

___ I might party on Saturday nights, but I try to make it to church on Sunday mornings.

___ I think of a relationship with God as an important part of the good life. I can sometimes put that on the same level of importance as finding the right person to marry, finding the right job, and building a great family.

___ If I'm honest, I get more upset when I can't have sweet tea, coffee, football, hunting, fishing, and/or grits than I do when I can't make it to church.

___ I get upset when people try to take prayer out of school, but I have rarely prayed while in a school.

___ I can easily quote lyrics to my favorite country music songs, but I cannot quote the Ten Commandments.

___ Total

The Picture Day Mullet

___ I am happy to cook a meal for someone who is hurting, but I don't want to invest emotionally or spiritually. I like to keep my distance from others in need.

___ I work hard to keep up the appearance that I have my life together and I don't need anyone or anything.

___ I claim and believe promises from the Bible that I've never really studied. To be honest, I have never read the verses before or after, but the promise sure looks good on my coffee mug, bumper sticker, social media feed, etc.

___ The family our church sees on Sunday is night-and-day different from the family we are the rest of the week.

___ I can never imagine allowing anyone into my home or life without making sure everything looked presentable first.

___ **Total**

The Slater Mullet

___ I don't think it is a big deal for teenagers and young adults to have a few lustful thoughts and actions. Boys will be boys and people need to sow their wild oats before settling down.

___ I think it's perfectly fine for young children to have special boyfriend/girlfriend relationships. I often encourage children to be boyfriend and girlfriend.

___ My biggest concern for my kids dating life is that they don't end up pregnant or getting someone pregnant.

___ I'm not too concerned about my son being sexually active as long as it's with girls and not boys.

___ I don't think I should have anything to do with the dating process for my kids. They need to figure it out.

___ **Total**

The 'Dega Mullet

____ I just want Jesus; don't give me any of that theology stuff.

____ I think about Jesus on Christmas and Easter, but he doesn't come to mind much on the other 363 days of the year.

____ I asked Jesus into my heart years ago, and that's all the religion I need.

____ I rarely pray other than saying grace around the dinner table.

____ I cannot imagine going more than a few days without coffee or sweet tea or sugar or TV or social media, but truthfully Jesus, His Word, and His church are not on that list.

____ Total

The Joe Dirt Mullet

____ My church is in the deer stand, on a boat, or in my recliner at home.

____ I don't do organized religion.

____ I spend more time on my hobbies than I do with my family.

____ Kids are a hassle, and I can't see why anyone would want a big family.

____ I don't really go to church that often. When I do, I get in and out as quickly as possible. If I'm lucky, I get a good nap in while I am there.

____ Total

How did you do? If you scored eleven or higher on any section, it's time for a haircut!

About the Authors

Derek and Lindsay Allen have served in ministry together since they were teenagers. They met as Summer Missionaries in 2000 and were married in 2003. They have five children—Jackson (born 2008), Meredith (born 2010), Sawyer (born 2013), Elizabeth (born 2017), and Marshall (born 2020). Derek and Lindsay spent seven years as church planting missionaries in Miami, Florida with the North American Mission Board. Currently they serve at First Baptist Tillman's Corner in Mobile, Alabama, where Derek is the Senior Pastor. The Allens host a podcast called "The C2 Life" where they discuss a variety of real-life issues from a Christ-centered worldview.

Derek has a Bachelors in Psychology from Jacksonville State University, a Masters of Divinity from New Orleans Baptist Theological Seminary, and a Ph.D. in Organizational Leadership from the Southern Baptist Theological Seminary. He is currently in the writing stage of a Ph.D. in New Testament from Midwestern Baptist Theological Seminary. Derek enjoys dating his wife, playing with his kids, reading, writing, running, and playing basketball.

Lindsay has a Bachelors in Education from Auburn University and is a stay at home mom. She enjoys homeschooling her five children and dating their dad often.

Other titles from Derek and Lindsay:

Trading Walls for Altars, Lindsay Allen
How to Love the Bible, Derek Allen

Both books, along with podcasts, sermons, Bible studies, and articles are available at thec2life.org.